FROM HOUSE TO HOUSE

A Manual on Personal Work

by

Ivan Robert Stewart

Evangelist
Church of Christ

Copyright, 1956

Second Printing
(10,000 Printed)

Old Paths Book Club Edition
Box V
Rosemead, Calif.

Printed by
Firm Foundation Publishing House
Austin, Texas

DEDICATED TO

my faithful wife, known affectionately to all as Polly, and my three lovely children: Sharon Rae, Michael Ivan, Rebecca Sue and to a host of faithful Christians with whom I have had the privilege to study.

TABLE OF CONTENTS

TABLE OF CONTENTS (Continued)

Preface

I do not claim to be an author, nor to present herein a masterpiece, but only to share some of my experiences with those who are working hard to restore New Testament Christianity. The aim is not to present deep thoughts, but suggestive material to inspire more people to take the simple gospel truths from house to house. It is my hope this book will help others in converting precious souls from the power of darkness that God may translate them into the Kingdom for their soul's eternal salvation. Originality is not the aim in this book, but since little is in print on the subject of personal evangelism, I want to present that which is common property and available to all, but arranged in such a nature to cause people to open the Bible and read God's truth for themselves, and thus to be more ready to accept it. Many could have written a better book, but upon the insistence of brethren that have known my work, I have undertaken this task, and perhaps it will give rise to better works in this area of endeavor. I am grateful to the educational institutions where I have studied, and to my teachers, both in those institutions and in private. The following persons have helped me greatly with my obedience and growth: My wife, the late J. Emmett Wainwright, Floyd Thompson, the late Morgan Harlan, Fred Walker, W. B. West, Jr., and the elders wherever I have labored. I am especially grateful to the late Morgan Harlan, who was the first to encourage me to study privately with people and gave me many helpful ideas. I am also very thankful to Brother Frank Pack and Brother Willard Collins for taking the time to read the manuscript and to offer valuable suggestions. Of course there are many others to whom I am deeply indebted, but space will not permit me to identify all of them by name. Many authors have used much of the material presented herein, and specific credit would be given to much more of it if the original source were known. The illustrations and points used have either been read, heard from professors and preachers, or experienced, and are presented here as common property—just as the material has been presented to help me—even so I present it to help others. I am thankful to God for my religious experiences and for life itself within which to work out my salvation, and am also humbly grateful for whatever time and ability He has granted me in helping others to study. May God bless your reading and effectual working of this method that you may help many others to obey the gospel.

Ivan R. Stewart
Albuquerque, New Mexico
August, 1956

TWO MONTHS LATER

This writer is humble and thankful for the wonderful reception given the first printing. It has been received so well that the second printing was required in less than 60 days. Interest in personal work is also demonstrated by the fact that many congregations have already begun using the book as a text and during this short period, one college has indicated it will be used as a text and Abilene Christian College has invited me to teach on the subject in the 1957 Lectureship. I am looking forward to this hoping to help others do this wonderful work. Brethren everywhere have expressed their thanks that there is at last a book that spells out the process step by step rather than giving the theory. They have written their thanks for writing material that is nowhere duplicated in any other book. It is too early, but no doubt time will tell of the true value when congregations begin baptizing and restoring many as a result of men and women loving the lost and preparing themselves so they can do something about it. A sincere thanks and may God continue to bless all in this field of endeavor.

Ivan R. Stewart

Introduction

How often, even after years of Bible study, church attendance, and prayer, do we feel inadequate in leading souls out of darkness into the glorious light of the gospel. Brother Ivan Stewart has made a realistic study of doctrinal and tactical obstacles which stand in the way of our converting people to Christ, or of leading them to a clearer understanding of New Testament Christianity. It has been my privilege to see and hear Brother Stewart actually apply the principles included in FROM HOUSE TO HOUSE in personal interviews with prospects. From observation of his methods and Scriptures used, and from reading the manuscript of the book, I consider it one of the most down-to-earth, yet thorough and Scripturally sound methods of studying the Bible with a person with the specific end in view of leading that person to obey the gospel.

FROM HOUSE TO HOUSE seeks to remedy a gap in our teaching and a deficiency in our methods of approach. It is a most flexible system of presenting pertinent Scriptures in that one may deviate from the "Main-track Scriptures" at will to deal with any question of truth or error that arises, using one's own supplementary references as "Sidetrack Scriptures." It supplies the personal worker, not only with appropriate Scriptures, but also with apt illustrations and questions which keeps the interview moving toward the desired objective: a positive decision for Christ.

The chapter, "Some Closing Appeals over Objections" alone is worth the price of the book. Much of the hesitancy of the average Christian to attempt personal work is due to his remembrance of ticklish questions about and formidable objections to the church of Christ which have been presented to him in previous attempts. Such an experience places a mental block on some Christians for life, yet a diligent study of methods of successfully winning souls to the Lord, and a patient application of these principles early in their Christian life, would have given them the necessary confidence to become ardent personal workers for Christ. Long have we needed a course of study for new converts which will capture that first blush of enthusiasm for the Lord and solidify it through the months into an eternal flame for the truth in the heart of the Christian.

Brother Stewart is admirably suited for the work he has done by the scholarly energy he possesses and by his own search for the truth before obeying the gospel under the teaching of J. Emmett Wainwright, in San Diego, California, on December 21, 1945. Born on October 24, 1922, into a family with Catholic, Methodist and Christian Church background, Ivan's real religious interest was not stimulated until he married Pauline Copher in 1944. She, by her determined, but patient insistence on regular church attendance, helped her husband to see that there was really a difference in churches. Meanwhile, he served six years in the Navy and was felled by the concussion of one of the first bombs dropped on Pearl Harbor on the fateful day of December 7, 1941. Though having the rating of Chief Storekeeper at the war's end, he felt the necessity of preparing himself to teach the word of God more effectively and of making this his life's work. His wife, Polly, applauded this decision but was stricken with tuberculosis at this time and spent two and one-half years in bed, most of that time in the hospital. Undaunted by this misfortune and with faith in God, Ivan forged ahead and went to college, selling shoes and preaching when he could. He received his Bachelor of Arts degree after studying with three educational institutions: George Pepperdine College, Los Angeles, California; University of California at Berkeley, California; and Abilene Christian College, Abilene, Texas. After laboring in Southern California,

Brother Stewart and family moved to the Washington, D. C., area to work with the West Hyattsville, Maryland congregation. It was here this writer became acquainted with him and observed his methodic manner of interviewing prospects with a reading of "Main-track" Scriptures. Brother Stewart served as a teacher in our Skyline Bible Camp near Front Royal, Virginia. Some of those whom he helped to convert are faithful members of the Arlington, Virginia congregation where I labored prior to coming to Chattanooga.

Brother Stewart is now in his third year of a successful ministry with the Netherwood Park Church of Christ, Albuquerque, New Mexico, and is the author of a unique Bible correspondence course of six lessons. Within six months after it was offered, over 8000 students in America and several foreign countries had enrolled in it.

Knowing something of the success of Brother Stewart's methods with those who will study with him, I have encouraged him to publish this arrangement of Scriptures, together with the method and wording by which he presents them. (He conservatively estimates that he baptizes one out of every four with whom he studies by this method). Surely the Lord is pleased when we take the gospel in a more personal way to souls in darkness at our very doors. Our gratitude goes to Brother Ivan Stewart for this simplified, yet successful means of teaching our neighbors the Truth.

Fred B. Walker
Chattanooga, Tennessee
1956

HOW TO USE THIS BOOK

Many individuals may desire to study this volume and prepare themselves in the art of studying with others privately. This can be accomplished out of the classroom situation by beginning at the front of the book and continuing through Chapter VII thoroughly and prayerfully. Do not proceed to the next section until each Chapter is thoroughly understood. It is unwise to go to any section of the book and strive to use it unless all previous sections have been covered. After the individual has completely read the book, he will then want to return and use certain sections for easy reference on the problem confronting him.

Many congregations and groups of Christians will want to prepare themselves for this great work by preparing in the class situation. In every instance, each student should have a copy of the book and pursue it ultimately as suggested above. The material that needs to be referred to often is so arranged for easy reference. Though the teacher may defer some of the material to private study, it does not mean that that material is the least necessary. In studying with others we study so as to be "ready always to give answer to every man that asketh you a reason concerning the hope that is in you" (1 Pet. 3:15). In order to do this we must study each section carefully.

There is more material presented in this book than can be covered in most classes due to the limitation of the duration of the class. If a class could be arranged for 24 to 36 class periods all material should be covered in the classroom. When the class can be taught only for 10 to 16 periods, the following suggestions will be helpful. When the teacher cannot cover a section, the teacher should encourage the students to read and study carefully the section omitted. It is wise for the teacher to take the part of the objectioner when discussing approaches to show the right and wrong. The teacher and student will discover that most of the time our answer causes arguments and that is what we desire not to do. The same procedure should be true of "Closing Appeals Over Objections." A few basic examples to the class will give them an opportunity to see how to study out of the classroom. Toward the end of the study, one period should be devoted to showing how an actual study is conducted. The ideal is to take the student with you, one or two at a time, to an actual study, but since many studies do not lend themselves to this, a "practice period" is suggested, to help the students become familiar with the manner of study. The teacher should be the personal worker and some student could pretend he is a member of a domination. Go through the actual study Scriptures with this set-up. As the students have actual study appointments, have them report back to the class so that they may have their work analyzed. The chart suggested in the chapter "Method of Actual Study" will assist in making the report and analysis.

CHAPTER I—THE RESTORATION PLEA The importance of personal work is shown in this chapter and every student should know this first. This should be discussed in highlight form during the first sessions of the class. It is possible to use some of the material as suggestive material for sermons to instigate the program or instill a desire in the members to do this type of work.

CHAPTER II—THE PERSONAL WORKER This chapter deals with the personal worker's early preparation and attitudes. Some attitudes need to be changed. Overcoming excuses is a must to make better personal workers. If time does not permit, it might be suggested that the section "Overcoming Excuses" be studied privately, but in the order presented in the book. Cover the rest of this chapter thoroughly in class.

CHAPTER III—GETTING THE APPOINTMENT. This chapter should be presented to the class. In discussing "Approach Problems" present the basic problems and solutions and suggest the whole section be digested thoroughly at home if not enough time is available in class. Since appointments are usually very hard for the beginner to make, it is suggested that the more experienced make appointments for the beginner at first, or at least help him in making them. Appointments properly made assist the individual greatly in accepting the gospel truths.

CHAPTER IV—METHOD OF ACTUAL STUDY. Cover this chapter thoroughly in class. It is preferable that the "Don't" section be discussed but if a section must be left out due to lack of time, this would be the suggested section, however, discuss several of the "Don'ts" to assist in private study.

CHAPTER V—CLOSING. Discuss all of this chapter in class and the basic manner of closing as presented in "Closing Appeals Over Objections."

CHAPTER VI—PREPARING THE INDIVIDUAL TO ACCEPT THE BIBLE AS THE WORD OF GOD. Since most personal workers will deal with those who are religious but wrong, it is suggested that this section be presented in the classroom only if time permits. It is easier to begin by having study periods with people who accept the Bible as the only authority. This is not always possible to ascertain before entering into a study, but in most cases it is.

CHAPTER VII—THE SCRIPTURES. Have the students mark their Bibles as suggested in this chapter out of the classroom, but go over each Scripture and the questions thoroughly in the class period. The section on "Restoration and Withdrawal" is intended for the assistance of elders or those assigned to this important work. Do not present this section in the classroom.

CHAPTER VIII—FOLLOW-UP. It is not necessary to cover this in the classroom. Personal workers do not necessarily have to do this work, but should understand it so as to prepare the prospective Christian or the newborn babe concerning the fact that they must grow. The personal worker should especially offer the guidance available in the congregation and also introduce them to the elders who "watch in behalf of your souls, as they that shall give account" (Heb. 13:17). The elders have the oversight of the follow-up program and should provide the best possible. EVERY CONGREGATION SHOULD HAVE A FOLLOW-UP PROGRAM.

CHAPTER IX—OFFICE PROCEDURE. It is not necessary to cover this in the classroom. Again, personal workers do not necessarily do this work. They may assist in it or use it to great advantage. Elders in every congregation should have an office procedure—some simple and some more elaborate.

BIBLIOGRAPHY. This section is intended to provide private instruction to the personal worker so that he can further improve himself and assist the new convert to walk the new life. Congregations would do well to have most of these books in the "church library."

THE RESTORATION PLEA

The Plea Itself

The Restoration plea is a good one. The plea of honest people should always be to restore Christianity to the pattern delivered in the New Testament. To accomplish this, we must speak where the Bible speaks and remain silent where it is silent. For the most part, we are striving and succeeding in carrying out that plea, which is a Scriptural plea. The plea can very well be used in carrying the gospel from house to house. Just a reformation or a change is not sufficient when a complete restoration is possible. It is possible to worship God today as He was worshipped about 2000 years ago because we have the pattern. It is possible to evangelize the world today as it was years ago because we have examples and a pattern given in the same Book that tells us how to worship and gives the right plan of salvation.

Is the Restoration complete? Constant study and research is necessary for restoration. When you visit the home of George Washington in Mount Vernon, Virginia, you will notice that an effort has been made to restore every item to its original state. As you travel through it, it appears to conform to the historical pattern you read in history years ago. It seems as if the restoration of this estate is complete, yet there are a number of people constantly studying and researching, trying to restore it, if need be, closer to the actual time of George Washington. Many brethren with kindred minds have endeavored to restore the church of our Lord Jesus Christ to be just as it was when it was established. A constant study and research reveals that the part most often left undone is that of the private personal presentation of the gospel. We know and practice well public preaching. Why? Because the Bible gives an example. The same Bible gives exam-

ples of private presentations, and we should know and
practice well that phase also. This plea is to add and restore to the pulpit and class presentation of the gospel the
private presentation with an open Bible. In our mind's
eye, we might think Mt. Vernon is as near perfect as can
be to the original pattern. The same may appear to many
regarding the present methods of evangelism, yet we need
to have a restoration movement begin with personal work.
Certainly there are many phases of personal work—but
this phase is of that regarding private study, "guiding"
people into a proper "understanding" and application of
what they have read for years.

Many will say "Amen" but still not do much about it.
We have heard a lot on personal work in recent years, and
too many have the idea it is just visiting socially, whereas
the Bible teaches us not only to be hospitable, but to teach
so as to win souls. Some lack a method to do this work
and the majority lack the effort which it takes to practice
any method. Brother Hailey said it like this: "The cause
cannot be attributed to the plea, for the plea is right;
therefore it must be located in the method or lack of method in doing the work, or in holding to a method that does
not meet the demands of this age. Possibly the failure is
due to lack of effort after any method." **Let's Go Fishing
For Men,** Page 3. If we will restore the method of individual teaching, and use the effort that it takes to make
it work, we will see many more souls being won to Christ
and they will be better taught. This work will be devoted
toward making the Scriptural method clear, and of course
there must be a beginning place. Should we desire to make
a trip around the world, we must first learn the way, and
second, take the beginning steps or we will never take the
final steps to complete the journey. If Christians will
take the first step in studying with others, they will continue because of the results they see.

The Plea itself is based upon the Scriptures. Acts 20:20 reads, "And now I kept back nothing that was profitable unto you, but have shewed you, and have taught you publicly, and **from house to house**". A restudy of every Christian practice should be made and a restoration made of preaching "from house to house". The book of Acts shows us how the apostles evangelized on the individual basis. Specifically, Acts 5:42 reads, "and **daily** (not just Sundays and Wednesdays—IRS) in the temple and **in every house**, they ceased not to teach and preach Jesus Christ." Individuals preached as they were spread about the world— Acts 8:4. "They (individuals—IRS) that were scattered abroad went everywhere preaching the word." Philip preached Jesus to one individual, the Ethiopian eunuch in Acts 8. Peter worked with one morally and spiritually devout family in Acts 10. There is no indication that just the specially trained evangelists did this work. Even in the writings to the churches the emphasis is upon the personal evangelization of the communities. Philippians 2:14-16 states, "Do all things without murmurings and disputings: that ye may be blameless and harmless, the sons of God, without rebuke in the midst of a crooked and perverse nation, among whom ye (individuals—IRS) shine as lights (individual—though plural—IRS) in the world, holding forth the word of life." It was not the special-classed, trained teachers, but the brethren that spoke the word. In Philippians 1:14 we read, ". . . many of the brethren in the Lord (at Rome—IRS), waxing confident by my bonds, are much more bold to speak the word without fear." God's way succeeded then and will succeed today. God spoke often of individuals being "lights of the world". Let us be lights instead of depending upon the preachers and each one of us practice personal evangelization more and more and thus bear more and more fruit as was borne in the first century.

What Will Personal Work Accomplish?

Personal work will accomplish what many other efforts will not accomplish. Personal work will accomplish on a personal level what public work will not accomplish. The pulpit will reach many that personal work will not. That is the reason BOTH are needed. Personal contact and personal application of the Scriptures are appreciated by most with whom you study. In the public situation, the individual may be thinking about things many miles away or even making an application of the Scriptures that is not intended. A preacher held a meeting for us one time. His subject was "Saved by Faith" based on Ephesians 2:8. This was a Scriptural sermon and my brother did an excellent job. At the door, a refined lady complimented the preacher and said that the sermon was just like the sermon her preacher would preach, stating that she attended the Baptist Tabernacle on Main Street. Of course the preacher was aghast that she had not digested the sermon. In a private study period, it would have been simple to show that Baptists teach "faith only" and that is a long way from "grace through faith", and the lady could have read the Scriptures herself under such conditions, but it was difficult to do so at that time. In personal work, the error could have been detected and pointed out because she could have read for herself that which was wrong and could have seen that which was right. It is better, so to speak, to have God say it direct to them on the printed page than for you to quote it to them.

Personal work does not leave the individual untaught. It does not appeal to the emotions only, but answers every question the student of God's word may ask—both positive and negative and in contrast to things right and wrong. If we teach only those things that are right, we have failed to "rebuke or correct" and the individual does not know from what he should turn. We must remember that

repentance is a command and that a complete change from
error to righteousness is required. Luke 13:3; Acts 17:30;
2 Cor. 7:10. Personal private study, both before baptism
and afterwards, helps to teach individuals the necessary
truths of the gospel. A lady attended services in a certain city, answered the invitation and was baptized, then
asked, "What church can I join now?" Certainly she was
untaught and a few private study periods would have
helped her understand more completely the gospel she was
attempting to obey. Many obey the gospel and completely ignore the opportunities to study in the Bible School.
One individual that answered the invitation one morning
without previous study privately and evidently without
much study publicly, did not know that she was obligated
to partake of the Lord's Supper. During a personal study
you can cover every subject necessary to begin the Christian life on a good foundation.

**Personal work will strengthen the individual for con-
tinued faithfulness after baptism.** It has been my experience that those taught on the personal level remain more
faithful because they know it has been applied to them
personally. Of course an individual cannot be taught everything in just a few hours, but neither is he taught everything from the pulpit in just a few hours. The individual is made aware of the necessity of further study
and he usually makes a personal application of other lessons too, as he did when you studied with him privately.
Let me illustrate the point. A few years ago it was my
privilege to study with a Doctor who believed there was
no God and in the evolution theory. After a few hours of
study each week over a period of two months, he decided
to obey the gospel. Of course he had come a long way,
but by no means did he know everything. One day in Bible study we were studying the sin of dancing. He told
the class that he had never seen that before and certainly

wanted to know if it were right or wrong. He did study further and made a personal application of the lesson.

The private study period allows the student to cover more material in a few hours than can be covered in many hours of preaching. One day a man told me that he had learned more in two hours of private study than he had learned in three years of listening to preaching. That may be true, and it is equally true that what he had learned previously had not meant as much to him—that he was not making a personal application of it—prior to the private study period or he would have obeyed sometime during the three years prior to the study period.

Personal work allows God's teacher to appeal for action. It is true that you can appeal for obedience from the pulpit but not as personal as when just two or three are present with an open Bible before them. Personal work places the teaching situation on a warmer and closer level. Many times on the personal level, you can find the hindering cause for postponement of obedience, while in other types of teaching situations you cannot. Recently I studied with a man and he agreed with everything that was presented from the open Bible but refused obedience. After several questions he told me why he could not be baptized. He told me he was too mean and had committed sins that no one would forgive, not even the Lord. I turned to 1 John 1:9 and had him read it. After a few minutes of fervent study, he then said, "I will let the Lord forgive me of all my sins."

Personal work will assist in the restoration of the way-ward as well as give instruction to the individual for entrance into the church. James 5:19-20 reads, "Brethren, if any of you do err from the truth, and one convert him; let him know, that he which converteth the sinner from the error of his way shall save a soul from death, and shall hide a multitude of sins." The same process of presentation, that of personally presenting the truth, will draw attention to the Scriptures concerning the wayward and make an appeal for a change of life. Many individuals need to be told of their lack of faithfulness and need for a change. This is a very difficult situation and is best handled by letting the individual see what God has to say to him concerning his soul's salvation. Personal work will give instruction which is needed for growth and strength in the Lord.

Converts from the private study periods stay converted. Years ago, many were converted who have since fallen away. Most of them either had not studied enough before conversion, or did not continue studying after conversion. If we ourselves are sincerely interested in the Christ who hung on the cross for us, we will take the time to study and prepare ourselves that we may so present the gospel privately to others, that those who are converted today will be avid learners, and continue zealously working for the Lord. We need to re-enter areas and work and work, but this time using also the personal application of the Scriptures. So that none will misunderstand, I must say the pulpit and classes are a MUST—this is a plea to restore and add the personal individual method of teaching the gospel. The New Testament records more individual teaching situations than public. Let us begin recording the same things in the Lord's book of remembrance in Heaven. From the figures available, the majority converted after private study are remaining faithful and growing constantly.

Personal Joy Through Personal Work

Reward comes after work. The pay check comes after we have worked. The joy comes after accomplishments. When I was a small boy, I remember dreaming about certain tasks and would often go so far as to try to fulfill some of my dreams. I remember I thought an old sewing machine would make a fine jig saw. I tinkered and tinkered until one day I could make the treadle machine saw wood. Although crude and very far from practical, I settled back and thought with great joy about the accomplishment. Much more time was spent than necessary to travel to the store and much more money was spent than a small copen saw would have cost—but think of the joy after the task was completed.

Spiritual work and spiritual fruit should bring greater joy. Many school teachers, both grade school and college, look back after a few years to the pupil that succeeds, and with great joy have expressed their happiness that they have been permitted to assist that child become a success. The privilege of helping an individual so change his life as to escape the eternal fires should cause us to leap with greater joy. A few times the school teacher has worked only for the money involved and to fulfill a task to please men. In teaching the Bible, we can only think of pleasing God and certainly should not make money our god.

Personal joy comes from the one helped. To see the change that comes in the life of an individual is thrilling, and nothing brings tears to my eyes quicker than having someone write or tell me that they are so happy that I took the time out to bring them to a greater appreciation of God's word. This joy does not cease here but is carried on from generation to generation. Already, some of the children of people I have helped to obey the gospel are walking in paths of righteousness. If God permits me to live long enough, perhaps I'll see their children walking after the precepts of God and thus the joy never ceases.

Personal joy comes when one you have helped in turn helps others. We read in II Timothy 2:2, "And the things which thou hast heard of me among many witnesses, the same commit thou to faithful men, who shall be able to

teach others also." When you witness this coming to fulfillment and recognize that you have had a small part in
helping, having committed the teachings of Christ to others who in turn will teach, you cannot help but have great
joy. I baptized a man in California. Convinced he could
not continue in the work in which he was then engaged,
and serve God acceptably, he left his position and traveled
to another city. Upon his arrival, he discovered that there
were no saints worshipping together at that place. He was
deeply concerned and after several days of making contacts
with various persons in the community, he advertised in
the local newspaper and began holding meetings in a private residence. Six were present at the first meeting. As
time went on, as many as fifty people appeared for services.
He preached Christ unto them and many realized their need
and were restored. He preached and did much personal
work with the people and at the end of the first year four
had been baptized. At the present time, a full time evangelist is engaged and they have built with their own hands
a beautiful new meeting house. This man has many talents
and thanks God for his ability to have been able to design
the building and contribute his means and leadership ability
in the growth of this fine work. This is truly a great personal joy.

**Personal joy comes when you see God fulfilling his prom-
ises.** Paul expressed this joy somewhat in I Corinthians
3:6, "I have planted, Apollos watered; but God gave the
increase." When God gives the increase because we have
planted and watered it should give us great joy. You
might ask, "Why"? Simply because God will not give increases where we have not taught properly His will. This
should be joy beyond measure of expression.

**Personal joy comes when you have been persecuted be-
cause of teaching God's Word.** Matthew 5:10-12 demonstrates to us that we are "blessed" if we have been per-

secuted for His sake. This blessedness should be our joy. Not all with whom you study will accept the teachings as you have presented them from God's Book—some will turn and talk and strive to slander your good work. They will twist and try to misrepresent things that you have said and try to make a personal injury toward you. Jesus did not make followers of all that He contacted and certainly some turned on Him, trying Him, perverting, and ridiculing Him until ultimately He was crucified on the cross—Question: Was that death on the cross a joy for Christ?

Personal joy comes when we realize we are carrying out the great commission as given in Matthew 28:18-20. Every Christian is a preacher (I Peter 2:9) and every Christian has the responsibility to carry out every command Christ has given. Personal work is a marching order of Christ and must be used to "teach all nations." **Multiplicity in personal work brings a joy as to the combined results.** If every congregation would train just ten personal workers and each one of them would study with just one person a month, and if they baptize one out of every four with whom they study, then each congregation would save forty souls through their efforts each year. If there are 15,000 congregations, as someone has estimated, then 600,000 souls could be saved every year and then repeat and repeat the process. Question: Are we doing that well from the pulpit? Wouldn't that be great joy this side of heaven?

Personal joy comes when personal work is exercised in the family relationship and whole families walk uprightly. Noah saved his family—do you think he had joy in his heart when he heard that God told him just his family would be saved and that not a one of them would be lost? He was not happy because others were lost, but certainly he could be happy about his own family. A young Christian about 30 years of age recently told me he had never converted anyone to Christ and was looking forward to the day when he could see his children obey the gospel. It is wonderful that a Christian father looks to saving his household, and may I say that if that is all he ever helps to save he will be a happy man, but he does not have to wait until his children are old enough to begin doing personal work and he can have the joy long before then. Far too many families are not even saving their own families. Think of the great joy as contrasted to the heartaches and sorrow when they do not obey. Personal work will help you in studying with your own family also.

The personal joy at the time of obedience is not all the joy that is to be had. Think of the joy you give others. A man was baptized one weekday evening. A few weeks later letters were received from many of his relatives in distant States because they were so happy time had been taken to study with this man. Not a few times, a man has been baptized and a wife and children in tears of joy have demonstrated their happiness to the obedient soul with a big hug and kiss. When I travel, people who are related or friends of others that have been helped through private study question me and express their joy to me. It is an unending process and once you have experienced the deep inner satisfaction that comes with helping one person understand the gospel and obey it, you will never want to stop studying with people.

Lack of conversion does not cause joy. One of our dearest friends, an elderly lady who traveled to California with her husband in a covered wagon years ago, has many times, with her eyes brimming with tears, said to me, "My husband was such a good man, so kind and honest to everyone —oh, if someone had just taken the time to come and talk with him when he was in the back yard, whittling." It takes time to go to a person and interest him in wanting to study, and more time in actually opening the Bible and studying, but are our lives our own? Aren't they just loaned to us by God for a while and even though it seems like a great amount of time is necessary to convert just one individual, don't we still have a lot of hours in each day to care for ourselves?

Joy is illustrated in the Bible concerning obedience. The place of joy is important. Does it precede or follow obedience? Reread the conclusions of the conversions of the Philippian Jailor (Acts 16), the Ethopian eunuch (Acts 8) and Cornelius (Acts 10). It is truly a joy to witness the expressions of joy upon the faces of those obeying and their loved ones who are happy for them after they were stubborn and refused obedience until someone took a personal interest and studied with them privately with an open Bible, showing them where they were wrong. Truly, there is joy on the part of the teacher and on the part of the student and in heavenly circles.

One is a Good Audience

Large numbers do not have to be assembled to reap the harvest of souls for which the laborers are few. More individuals can be converted to Christ through this New Testament pattern than from all of the pulpits. Pulpit work is a must; however, personal work is needed in addition to it. Wherever personal work is not practiced, a restoration of it is needed. It has been my experience that 75% of those converted wherever I have labored are converted after a private study period with an open Bible. It is possible to convert one out of every four with whom you study. Imagine an audience where twenty-five are subject to the gospel invitation and six respond every time. The percentage is not that high in the audience situation— else six would respond out of that group after every sermon.

There is no competition in the field of personal work. The laborers are few today as they were in New Testament times. (Matthew 9:37). Teaching one man is a good audience. Many young men dream of the foreign mission fields, knowing full well they may never go overseas, but a mission field lies at every back door—a precious soul—not in the Kingdom of God. Many young women dream of marrying a preacher knowing full well they may not, but they can win souls to Jesus Christ by doing personal work.

Examples showing that one is a good audience are numerous. Insurance companies consider one or two individuals a good audience. They train their salespersons to spend long hours with those who will listen and reason. Appliance companies consider one or two individuals a good audience. Car salesmen consider one family a good audience. All of this is for a monetary value. An insurance company, an appliance company or an automobile company would go broke by constructing a building and advertising "come." Many of these companies do allow "floor time" where the people do come, but they also have "out time" where the salesperson "goes" directly to the home. Jesus considered one individual a good audience on certain occasions. He talked to and taught the woman of Samaria, Nicodemus, Mary, the rich young ruler, Zacchaeus and others on the individual basis. Read John 3 and 4, Matthew 13, Luke 10 and 19. Paul considered one or a few a good audience because he taught Felix, Agrippa, Festus and the Philippian Jailor. Read Acts 16, 24, 25 and 26. Peter found a whole family to be a good audience when he taught Cornelius and his family. Acts 10.

Have you ever experienced the joy that comes with helping with one soul to Christ? We dream of large numbers but one soul is precious and that soul may never respond to the Lord's invitation out of a large number of people if he does not make a personal application of the commands of Jesus. Have you ever cried or laughed for joy because you had a part in winning a soul to Christ? If you are a Christian, you should have. All of the joy that comes

with the saving of the souls of men does not have to be
reserved for the preacher. The preacher is not selfish in
this. Christians have the responsibility to preach as well
as the paid evangelist.

If you ever convert a soul to Christ, you will never want
to stop doing this kind of work. Many Christians have said
to me that they do not know what it means to help someone come to Christ. Every Christian should know that
joy. Every Christian should bear that kind of fruit. It
is a good thing and good things should be repeated. Individuals that taste good things such as food, fine cars,
fine clothes—desire a repeat performance. Here is the
finest thing in the world—the salvation of the souls of
men. Helen Young wrote recently on motherhood saying
that "as you look into the face of your first baby and
realize that you have cooperated with God in the creation
of this new life, this new soul, you are embarking upon a
marvelous new career." As the individual cooperates with
God in the presenting of the powerful Gospel, and witness-
ing obedience to it, he realizes with great joy that a soul
has been born into the Kingdom of God—saved from damna-
tion and delivered unto eternal life, a new life, a new soul,
a marvelous career.

One Lesson—not impossible today

How many lessons are needed today to prepare the individual for obedience? We note in the cases of conversion
recorded in the book of Acts that those who obeyed did so
as a result of only one or a few lessons. Recently, preachers have been saying that it takes 3000 sermons today for
each soul rather than one sermon for 3000 souls as recorded
in Acts 2. All know what this statement means—enough
can be learned in one lesson to enable people to obey the
gospel and begin the Christian life, if we will just apply
ourselves and help them to study.

There must be a reason why it takes more than one or a few lessons to convert people. Maybe the reason it seems to take 3000 sermons today is because we have grown to depend upon the pulpit and it alone in converting the souls of men and women and many think that is the only way that it can be done. It is true that Jesus preached to large multitudes but it is equally true that Jesus spoke on a number of occasions (which actually outnumber the public situations) directly to the individual or to small groups of individuals. If we will restore this example Jesus used, souls can be saved today as years ago, at the close of one lesson from the gospel. Certainly an individual should not be baptized that is not ready, but a private lesson dealing with the individual problems—properly presenting the errors of denominationalism, modernism, sensualism, materialism and showing the true witness of Christ from the Scriptures helps ready him for baptism. Any individual or congregation of individuals that says this is not possible denies that the Bible examples are for us today and generally is unwilling to follow the second half of the great commission which tells us to do something after baptism: "Teaching them to observe all things." There is more teaching yet to come after baptism. Certainly all baptized individuals are not polished Christians in their actions but they have a right to the tree of life if they continue to grow. In that respect, every congregation should have a program dealing with new converts to help them grow. A new-converts class will assist in this. A questionnaire or routine visit will determine their needs and progress. See the Chapter on "Follow-up" for a more thorough discussion of this project.

Some of the Bible examples should be noted to impress us with the effort to follow the Bible. The Bible demonstrates that it is possible to study with an individual and cause him to obey the gospel after only one lesson. Paul tried to persuade Felix and Agrippa to obey the gospel after

only one lesson. Paul did not refuse to baptize or persuade
people to become Christians after one lesson. Would you
refuse to baptize an individual who presented himself for
baptism—not knowing how many lessons he had had? Of
course you would not—how many sermons did he hear?
You do not know? Maybe just one? "You cannot baptize
after one lesson" is a statement that has been made. Where
is the authority for such a statement? The examples of
the New Testament show a better way of reasoning and
following, and it is much more reassuring to hear an individual assert his belief after a private study than to see
an individual walk down the aisle and wonder how much
he has been taught. We do not ask "How many sermons
or lessons have you heard?"—rather, "Is Jesus Christ the
Son of the Living God?" (Acts 8:36-40; Matthew 16:16).
Furthermore, we should be teaching publicly and privately
—obedience may come after either way and maybe after
just one or two lessons. The sooner an individual obeys,
if he is taught, the better, because we have no assurance
of another opportunity to hear another lesson.

**Personal private presentation cuts down the number
of lessons** needed and brings the soul into the saved relationship sooner. It is a known fact that usually people
listen to any number of public presentations in order to
cover the necessary materials that they desire to know
prior to obedience. Of course, one public lesson would be
enough if it covered enough material and if their hearts
were ready. The example of this is given in Acts 2 where
3000 obeyed. Certainly, more obeyed than could have had
there been private presentations—this is not a plea to limit
the pulpit but to add to that effort that which will reach
many who will not obey publicly. In the private session,
the individual may ask questions and receive the answer
immediately. Even when an individual has made up his
mind to obey, sometimes there are questions he still would
like to ask JUST TO BE SURE. In the public situation this

is not possible. Many people do not even know that we answer questions privately and thus do not seek an answer. Where preachers make it known they will study privately, they are swamped with opportunities. Very seldom do they have to go out seeking people with whom to study. Let us make a more concentrated effort to teach more Bible in private study periods, covering more ground in each lesson, so that people can obey and not die before they have had enough study to know what to obey.

Personal Work is More than a Social Visit

There are many mistaken ideas about personal work. It is presumed by many that personal work is a presentation of a watered-down gospel and therefore no one should attempt to do it. If the gospel is watered down in the pulpit, should faithful gospel preachers stop preaching? Of course not. Neither should faithful personal workers stop. It is wrong to water down the gospel in the pulpit or from a personal private presentation. The desire to win public favor is wrong whether it rears its ugly head in the pulpit or from the lips of an individual teaching another. Denominational teaching does not have its place anywhere in the world. You cannot take the blood out of the atonement privately nor publicly. You cannot take the inspiration out of the gospel privately nor publicly. No one can make a social gospel nor a social club out of God's teachings anytime anywhere and be pleasing unto God. The spirit of the teaching, the truth revealed in the gospel and the hope held in view in the Bible cannot be tampered with—whether it is private or public.

Personal work takes time. This may account for the reason preachers and members of the church do not do more personal work. Social visiting, which may or may not take a great amount of time, is sometimes called personal work. Social visiting is a work that is personal but so are many other works—such as selling automobiles and feeding the children. Actually, many social engagements must be foregone if you are to do this work effectively. The best hours are between 6:00 P.M. and 10:00 P.M.—that is the time when you can study privately with the most people. Are social activities more important than teaching a precious soul? No one can say YES. The personal work that we talk about is the private presentation of the gospel. It takes no less than one hour to present a gospel sermon from the pulpit. Do we expect every soul that will obey to do so just from public teaching? To those souls that will not learn and submit to the Lord's commands in a public teaching siutation, a personal persuasion is necessary and this usually requires several hours of someone's time. It takes time from another standpoint. When we present the gospel to an audience publicly we think that it takes only one hour at the most—that is for the public proclaimer. Actually, if 300 persons are present it takes 300 man hours. In contrast to the effort of the teacher to teach all 300 persons individually if they will not be taught publicly—allowing two or three hours for each person privately—it would take a lifetime. Therefore, the need is to teach more members of the church how to do personal work. Yes, it does take time.

Personal work is more than a social visit. Visiting may show your interest in the individual, which, of course, is a must. Cheering, comforting and showing interest may be accomplished by a social call, however, the instruction that is necessary to produce a saving faith cannot be accomplished in a few minutes—although it can be accomplished in a shorter time than many think. The book of Romans, Chapter 10, Verse 17, tells us that "faith cometh by hearing and hearing by the word of God." Therefore, telling people socially that you noticed they were at the services last Sunday and extending to them a welcome to return (and this is a must) will not cause them to hear nor produce a faith unless they do come back and listen to further ser-

mons. Comforting the sick and offering to assist them in
their time of need (and this is a must or we will not enter
the Kingdom of Heaven—read Matthew 25) does not cause
people to hear that which produces a saving faith. A social
call may be accomplished in a few minutes but a personal
study period may take many hours.

Personal Work

Religion is a personal thing. God did not design His way
so that some may work out the salvation of others. Philippians 2:12 says, "Work out your own salvation." First,
God did not Himself work it out for His creation. This is
quite obvious and certain when He revealed in Matthew
7:13-14 that the majority of mankind would not enter into
the narrow way for deliverance into the eternal Heaven.
We read in 2 Peter 3:9 that He was "not willing that any
should perish," yet He left it up to each individual to work
it out. Many personally will not accept God's way in spite
of God's desire and thus they will miss Heaven. God allows
man to be a free moral agent by inviting all to "come unto
me . . . and I will give you rest" Matthew 11:28. Since
God did not allow Himself to work salvation out for mankind, it is reasonable to notice that He would not allow
someone to work it out for another while upon the earth nor
after death, such as baptism for the dead or buying and
giving our good merits for those that have gone on before
us. Hebrews 9:27 tells us that our personal preparation
must be accomplished prior to death. "It is appointed unto
men once to die, but after this the judgment." (Not further time to prepare by the individual nor another time for
him to prepare).

Religion is a personal desire. The desire to be worthy
in the sight of a higher power has been true in every age.
This is so personal that it has divided families, the most
personal of all earthly relationships. One so keenly feels
the need to follow and the other so keenly feels that there

is no reason to follow. Even Jesus revealed this fact when
He revealed that the closest of relationships would be
divided by personal desire. Luke 12:52-53 states: "For
from henceforth there shall be five in one house divided,
three against two, and two against three. The father shall
be divided against the son, and the son against the father;
the mother against the daughter, and the daughter against
the mother; the mother in law against her daughter in law,
and the daughter in law against her mother in law."

Religion is a personal responsibility. When we read the
great commission we notice that it is a personal responsibility to carry out that commission. It was the personal
responsibility of Jesus to carry out the will of God. Jesus
could not transfer that work to another—neither can we
transfer, nor even purchase, the time of another to do that
which was intended that we should do.

Religion is spread on the personal basis. The teacher
of the Ethopian eunuch was in an individual teaching situation. The eunuch asked for personal guidance, "'How can
I except some man should guide me?" (Acts 8:31). II Timothy 2:2 teaches us that we are to spread the gospel to
others and then they in turn have the same personal responsibility to others. Jesus Christ called for individuals to
"come after" Him and He would make **them** fishers of men.
People often wonder why we do not convert large organizations if we have the truth. As the same basis of spreading
the news is by individuals, so is the conversion of people
by individuals, therefore it is the work of individuals. It
is true that the individuals making up the Lord's church
convert by mutual concentrated efforts, but it is equally
true that the work of each one of those individuals is important. Paul and Barnabas, though sent by the church
at Antioch, worked as individuals. Paul, in preaching the
gospel in his house at Rome, causes us to think that he
studied individually with people. At the judgment scene,

it will not be "What did the congregation do?" but rather
"What did YOU do?"

Work is a task assigned to God's people. God has designated man shall work and, whether it be serving tables or
teaching the word privately or publicly, none of these
assignments will be fulfilled by wishful thinking. They
will not be completed until we work at them. The emphasis that God places on work is demonstrated by the fact
that there are 619 references in the Bible using the word
"work." If we read these individual references in the
Bible we will note further the manner of accomplishing
God's will. God used individuals and many of their names
are recorded because they did the work of the Lord well.
The linking together of the two terms 'personal' and 'work'
tells us that the work of evangelism is of a personal application. Personal work is an individual effort to evangelize
as contrasted to congregational or united efforts. It is a
personal effort to study with a person, to cause him to
know from the Bible itself of a personal Saviour and to
persuade him to obey the truth so as to be personally saved
by Jesus Christ. The method of guiding the individual to
an acceptable understanding of God's Word presented in
this book is just one method among many, but it has worked
so well for this scribe that many have encouraged that it
be placed in book form to help others in the great work
of converting other people. If it helps just one person win
just one soul, I will have a heart filled with joy that this
work is not in vain.

THE PERSONAL WORKER

Why Be a Personal Worker?

There are a number of reasons for being a personal worker:

1. **This work imitates the work that Jesus Christ did.** The record of Jesus' life shows more individual teaching situations than public.   If we imitate just the public life, we have left undone a method of spreading the Kingdom. Teaching privately helps to declare the whole counsel of God, as Jesus Christ did.

2. **This work will seek and save the lost.** In Luke 19:10 we find that Jesus "came to seek and save the lost." A personal worker strives to find the lost.   Of course, an individual that is lost must allow himself to be found.   That is what the personal worker does. Personal work exposes error which causes one to be lost. It is effective.

3. **The personal worker obeys the commands given in the Bible.** Matthew 28:18-20, Mark 16:15-16 and Luke 24: 47-49 record the commission to go and preach, by way of command. The disciples understood it clearly in the first century.   It should be just as easily understood in all centuries. The commission still reads "Go and make disciples" not "Come and we will make disciples of you."

4. **The personal worker has a clear-cut example after which to pattern his work.** (Acts 20:20 and Acts 5:42). The same Bible that commands baptism gives the command to go and teach. The same Bible that gives examples of how to be baptized gives examples of how to go and teach privately and publicly.

5. **Every Christian should be a personal worker to help him bear fruit and save his own soul.** The Bible is clear that everyone cannot be a public teacher, but here is a work

that all can do and bear fruit. John 15:2 reads "Every branch in me that beareth not fruit, he taketh away: and every branch that beareth fruit, he purgeth it, that it may bear more fruit."

6. **It causes the personal worker to appreciate the power of God's Word for himself as well as others.** Certainly Romans 1:16 shows us that the gospel is powerful and it serves as a constant reminder to the worker of its power anew. Often I realize how feeble I am and how awkward with the presentation of God's Word, and yet the individual obeys anyway. This demonstrates to me that it is not me but the Word—but it must be presented. Personal work causes the Scriptures to be continually applied personally and not only to the other man. Personal work keeps the Christian busy. It will increase the effectiveness of the worker, helping him to grow spiritually and it will help the congregation, and in turn cause those converted to take up the task of converting others—thus more souls saved. The personal worker is working on the true values of life. See Mark 8:36: "What shall it profit a man if he shall gain the whole world and lose his own soul?" If you were receiving $10,000.00 for each convert, where would you place the value?

Overcoming Excuses

Excuses should not be connected with such a wonderful thing as the gospel. Christians should be soul winners, but it is astonishing to note that they put forth more excuses than effort many times. Those who do strive to win souls sometimes convert such a small number for the amount of effort. This, likewise, is covered up with excuses. All of this suggests that we need to help people put forth the effort, and second, help them to know the best effort to put forth. We need to learn a lesson from the lowly ant. In Proverbs 6:6 we read, "Go to the ant, thou sluggard; Consider her ways, and be wise." Since the gospel is sweet and wonderful and contains the only way by which we may reap the blessings of eternal life, we should not want to keep the message to ourselves, we should tell others of it in word and deed. Make this test: place a piece of sweetmeat away from other ants but with one ant on it. The ant will not eat alone but will absent itself and return with a long procession of ants to enjoy the morsel. The Christian may make many excuses for not proclaiming the gospel to others, but none will be justifiable.

Satan is working hard to help us make excuses that sound reasonable. Satan gave Eve an excuse to partake of the fruit of the tree of knowledge of good and evil. Satan helps the timid soul make excuses. He caused Moses to tell God he could not talk, but God provided a way superior to Satan's devices. Satan caused Jesus' disciples to "have little faith" when they were about to do the work of the Lord. Satan picks on us when we are weak. He picked on the Lord Jesus Christ when he had fasted for forty days and nights. Satan uses those of the inner circle (members of the church now) to accomplish his desires. Satan caused Judas to betray Christ and Peter to deny Him. The Devil is working with Christians today, striving to cause them to make light of the commands of the Lord to spread the gospel. He especially takes advantage of the untaught, the afraid, the sensitive and those that will make excuses for themselves not doing the Lord's work.

A glance at some of these excuses will show us how fruitless they are: Stumbling blocks must be removed before personal work can be effective. Let us help to remove some by analyzing them:

1. Jesus Christ taught us to analyze all excuses.

Read Luke 14:15-24. There are three excuses offered in this reading. (a) "I have bought a piece of ground, and I must needs go and see it: I pray thee have me excused." The fallacy of this excuse is that most men do not buy fields sight unseen, therefore, it was an excuse and not a reason. (b) "I have bought five yoke of oxen, and I go to prove them: I pray thee have me excused." The same fallacy exists with this excuse as the previous one offered. (c) "I have married a wife, and therefore I cannot come." Most men go where they want to with or without a wife. The final court of approval lies with the lord who has made the invitation, "For I say unto you, that none of those men which were bidden shall taste of my supper." These excuses are recorded that we may see the error of making excuses and the futility of trying to justify ourselves when we come face to face with spiritual opportunities. Other excuses are just as boldly advertised that men may also analyze them.

2. "I cannot do personal work." Analyze:

You can and should do personal work. If anyone can win a friend for himself —he can also win a follower to Christ. Would you admit that you could win friends to yourself and not to the greatest friend of all—Jesus? Maybe if we put forth the same amount of effort that we do in winning friends for ourselves—we would win them to Christ.

3. "I do not know how to do it." Analyze:

Can you learn to do other things? Have you ever baked a cake? Have you ever followed a pattern and made a dress? Have you ever typed a letter? Have you ever repaired a leaky faucet? Have you ever changed a tire? Most would answer "Yes" to some of these questions. Would we admit to God that we could learn about the things of this world that are sometimes more complicated than the things of God? Nat-

urally we do not know how if we do
not try to learn how.

4. "People do n o t
want to listen to
the Bible."
Analyze:

In many instances this may be true
but in many it is not. If some will not
listen—take it to others that do want
to listen. When I was a boy I did not
know of the church of Christ. A school
pal was a member of the church but
never mentioned it to me. Years later,
someone did talk to me about Christ
and I listened and obeyed. More are
willing to listen than are willing to tell
the old, old story—shame!

5. "I'll wait until I
learn all about it."
Analyze:

That day usually never arrives. Does
the apprentice carpenter wait until he
finishes the course to begin driving a
nail? If you arrived in Germany on
a vacation, would you wait until you
learned all the German language before you began using that language to
order food and make purchases? Your
vacation would be over before you
were able to buy anything. So will our
life on this earth be over if we wait
until we learn all about the Bible before beginning to tell others about it.

6. "I do not have the
time."
Analyze:

We have the time to do what we want
to do, both in learning how and in trying to do it. Matthew 6:33 tells us
to "seek ye first the kingdom of God"
and Matthew 6:21 tells us: "For where
your treasure is, there will your heart
be also." We usually make the time
for what we want to do badly enough.
One lady who claimed to be a Christian would repeatedly proclaim she did
not have time to come to the mid-week
services, but would just as regularly
attend the movies that evening with
her non-Christian husband.

7. "I'm already doing my part."
Analyze:

Since when does a man do all he can do when we think of ALL that Jesus gave? If we have the talent, we never have done our part. Maybe someone else is shirking his duty, but does that excuse us from ours? Maybe someone else does not do as much as you, but does that excuse you from doing more?

8. Odd but related excuse: "I have nothing to do since I have no class to teach."
Analyze:

Every Christian can have a very important class. The class may have only one student. Teaching does not have to be limited to the organized Bible School department. One Christian was not called upon to teach, but did have the talent. The elders had not learned of her good talents. She did not grumble but invited all of the children in the neighborhood into her home every Saturday morning for a Bible class. Others have gone out and taught their co-laborers, neighbors, etc. Teaching INDIVIDUALS is a WIDE OPEN FIELD.

9. "My husband works hard all day and gets home late. I attend two nights a week and think I should spend the rest of the time with him."
Analyze:

It is wonderful to note that families try to stay home once in awhile in these days—also to note that wives want to be in the company of their husbands, but no Christian should allow the non-converted to keep him from doing his Christian duty. If there is work to be done, maybe the wife needs to do her personal work in the daytime when her husband is working. If it cannot be done then, it must be done or we will be held accountable. The good work that she does is worth more than all the personal pleasure in his company. Sermons preached in our lives are the best sermons that others can hear. If a young Christian girl continues her work as a Christian immediately after marriage, her husband will want to go with her. This illustration might be in order. If a Christian wants to break her husband of drinking, can she do it by drinking with him a little? Even so, Christians convert others by our good work, and not our lack of it, and not by the participation in the sins of others.

10. "I have too many children and do not have enough time." Analyze:

If a mother recognizes her responsibility to children, it is commendable. She can still arrange her time so as to allow her children to help her, at least to not hinder her. If a mother wants to go other places, usually she arranges the time. We should consider our children God's blessings and not God's hindrances. God's children are like God's weather—good excuses for SOME. Parents should name their children "Excuse" rather than "Johnny" or "Susie", etc. Let this parent arrange to do the Lord's work as she does other things, and not let the children hinder this important phase of her life.

11. "I'm afraid I'll hurt somebody." Analyze:

Certainly if the way we do it causes us to hurt someone, then we ought to be afraid, but the individual who presents the gospel properly only to have the individual hurt should realize that Christ did not make all happy. To the rich young ruler He gave the instructions of what to do, but "he went away sorrowful." We need to learn the lesson in Hebrews 4:12, "For the word of God is quick and powerful, and sharper than any two-edged sword." We do not become offended when we ask people to go to a football game with us and they refuse, or when we invite them to dinner and they refuse. People need to be aroused to a certain degree to cause them to be "pricked" in their hearts to cause them to "repent and be baptized." Isn't that what we are supposed to do? To find the way to arouse them? Strive to touch the heart on purpose, not accidentally.

12. "I'm too old to learn," or "I'm just not smart enough."
Analyze:

This is an admission that should not be. Hebrews 5:12 states to them who make such excuses plainly, "For when for the time ye ought to be teachers ye have need that one teach you again which be the first principles of the oracles of God." If you are old, maybe you could do a very good work among others that are old. There is work to be done where there is talent, and there is work to be done where there is an opportunity. There is talent and there is opportunity as long as there is life. The average man only develops his mind 6%. There is room to grow. The Massachusetts Institute of Technology was quoted in the November, 1952 edition of Coronet Magazine thusly: "Scientists estimate that during a lifetime a man can store about 50 times more information than is contained in the 9,000,000 volumes of the Library of Congress." (Page 61) It is not so important that we retain everything we learn, but that we catalog it in our minds, to be able to know where to find the information studied when we need it again.

13. "I do not know where to begin."
Analyze:

Remember, if you wanted to begin in any other area badly enough, you would find out where to begin and work at it. Let us do the same thing here.

14. "I do not remember the Scriptures well."
Analyze:

The Lord admonishes us to study in 2 Timothy 2:15, and in numerous other places. The key word to the New Testament is Growth—and how are we to grow if we do not study? Again we could say we remember other things well. Why? Because we have trained ourselves. The chapter entitled "Scriptures" will help you to no longer make this excuse.

15. "I do not know enough to argue about it." Analyze:

In Acts 18:24-28 we learn that two individuals taught another one the way of the Lord more perfectly. Teaching should not be by bickering or wrangling, but presenting Bible arguments effectively is reasoning and discussing in such a way to cause individuals to see for themselves God's way. Underlying the excuse offered here is the absence of knowledge. Failure to gain it is violating a command of the Lord. Paul prayed for the church in Philippians 1:9, "I pray that your love may abound more and more in knowledge." Many times the underlying principle in such a statement is the fact that the individual has not built a good enough foundation upon which to stand; that is, he is afraid the other individual may prove him wrong. He needs to "prove all things and hold fast to that which is good."

16. "I do not have the right personality." Analyze:

If your personality hindered you in making a living, you would strive to improve it, wouldn't you? Would you do as much for the Lord? There is enough of your kind of personality with which to labor. It is odd that people have the personality to marry, to work with others, and to spend pastime with others, even to spend their whole life with others and not use the personality to help others spiritually. It is admitted that certain personalities do not work together, but there is always someone with whom you can work and study.

17. "I'm too tired."   Would you be too tired if someone of-
    Analyze: fered you $10,000.00 for each convert?
                            Would you be too tired if the soul you
                            saved belonged to your child, the one
                            you had watched over so very closely
                            and guarded physically for so many
                            years? Too often, we are not sincerely
                            interested in the souls of men.

Personal Preparation—Your Attitude

Many excuses are overcome by changing attitudes. In everyday life, we change our attitude and accomplish many tasks which seem to be almost impossible. This is all accomplished by necessity or the love that we can generate in our lives. If we could realize the necessity of not saying only "Lord, Lord", **but do the things that He has commanded,** we would accomplish many tasks for the Lord that seem almost impossible at first. If we can truly realize that it is a necessity of saving our own souls and the souls of others, and then realize the love that we have for God, we will be prompted to do ALL He has taught us we must do. John 14:15 reads, "If ye love me, keep my commandments," and in Philippians 4:13 we read, "I can do all things through Christ which strengtheneth me." Excuses never strengthened anyone, but the Lord will strengthen when we with love keep his commands—even bearing fruit when we think the situation is impossible for us to do personal work.

The personal worker's attitude toward the lost and dying world is important. Christians should love souls and especially lost souls. John 15:13: "Greater love hath no man than this, that a man lay down his life for his friends." Certainly allotting a few hours to study with a friend is not laying down your life for him, but it is better than taking no time out to talk to him at all. Love demonstrates the value we have for the soul of man. What do you see in an

individual when you think about his spiritual status? Do
you think here is a man who lives upon the earth that is
growing older and someday will be buried? Do you think
that it is none of your business to talk to him if he differs
with you? We should see in every temple (body) a precious soul that will spend eternity somewhere—either in
the presence of God or with the devil and his angels. Jesus
saw a soul in the woman at the well. He saw a soul that
was full of sin and unacceptable to God. His attitude was
that He must talk to her and that day. If some individual
felt he had the truth and you did not—wouldn't you want
him to tell you all about it? If you were living in sin, and
even though it might hurt your pride, wouldn't you want
to know it? God made man after His image, but notice
that the body was not a living soul until He breathed into
it the breath of life. It is that soul, that eternal part of
man, that lives on after the return of the body to the dust
from whence it came. If we see in man an eternal soul and
work with that soul, we have done a work that will endure
more than any other work. Why?—Because that soul saved
lives in eternity, immortal, not annihilated, without end.
That is the endurance of our soul-winning work. We cannot be like the newspaper reporter who called the mortuary
one day and asked the mortician, "Did anybody important
die today?" He thought people important only if they were
"headline material," but to the Christian, all souls are important.

Our attitude is reflected in our actions toward another
soul. Matthew 7:12 reads, "Therefore all things whatsoever ye would that men should do to you, do ye even so to
them; for this is the law and the prophets." If we argue
and wrangle, we can expect them to argue with us. If we
mention Christ to them in the right manner, we can expect
them to talk with the right attitude, too. If we allow them
to talk, then we can expect them to let us be the conversa-
tionalist at the right time. Someone has said a good conver-

sationalist must be a good LISTENER. If we listen, we can expect them to listen. II Timothy 2:24-26 states, "And the servant of the Lord must not strive; but be gentle unto all men, apt to teach, patient, in meekness instructing those that oppose themselves; if God peradventure will give them repentance to the acknowledging of the truth; and that they may recover themselves out of the snare of the devil, who are taken captive by him at his will." There are a number of attitudes that will be reflected properly or improperly toward another by our actions. We must not strive, but rather be gentle, meek, patient—yet instructing the gospel so that an individual will repent and acknowledge the truth. When Paul was talking with Agrippa, Festus and Felix, he reasoned with them and told them of their sins, but certainly there is no evidence that he quarreled with them.

Our attitudes will be reflected in our daily living. "If a man therefore purge himself . . . he shall be a vessel unto honour, sanctified, and meet for the master's use, and prepared unto every good work." (II Timothy 2:21). People in glass houses should not throw bricks. Christians that are not living the Christian life should not go forth proclaiming the word of God until they have straightened out their own lives. As Christians should love and live the Christian life, they should shine forth the happiness that Christ gives. Of cheerfulness and joy, Henry Ward Beecher wrote, "It is a light in the window of the face, by which the heart signifies it is at home and waiting. A face that cannot smile is like a bud that cannot blossom. Laughter is day and sobriety is night, and a smile is the twilight that hovers gently between both." Galatians 5:22-23 states, "The fruit of the Spirit is love, joy, peace, long-suffering, gentleness, goodness, faith, meekness, temperance." Let the Christian reflect this kind of fruit that will make others want to inherit the Christian life.

Our attitude must glorify Christ. We know that advertising is a must but in modern day advertising there is one famous exception to the rule. Hershey Chocolate Company does not advertise and has never spent a cent on advertising. We might ask, "How do they sell and continue to remain the number one chocolate seller in the country?" Good samples and consistency is the answer. The personal worker must also be consistent and give a good sample of his Christian living. Christ asked that his followers let their lights shine so that He may be glorified. People do not make a trail to your door unless they know what is there, therefore, we should so live that people will ask us to show them what is there—that is, what makes us the happy people we are. If we profess to be Christians but others know of the rotten kind of lives we live, we will not be able to feast with them upon God's word for they will excuse themselves. In Solomon 1:6 we read, "Look not upon me, because I am black, because the sun hath looked upon me: my mother's children were angry with me; they made me the keeper of the vineyards; but **mine own vineyard have I not kept.**" The Christian could very well adopt the following statement as his motto: "Be careful how you live, for you may be the only Bible some people ever read." In 1932, Camay soap advertised "You're in a beauty contest every minute of your life"—so Christians are in view of others with their lives. Sometimes the individual is prompted to be "on his toes," so to speak, just before the prospect with whom he is studying. Mark 12:28-34 brings to light that we live with people and that we should live neighborly at all times, "Thou shalt love the Lord thy God with all thy heart, and with all thy soul, and with all thy mind, and with all thy strength; this is the first commandment. And the second is like, namely this, Thou shalt love thy neighbor as thyself." No person is just going to love himself part of the time, therefore, as he loves himself all the time, let the Christian at all times live and love the Christian life. We will be assisted in reflecting good lights by other Scriptural teachings. Colossians 4:5 says, "Walk in wisdom toward them that are without, redeeming the time." When I first began preaching, I thought truly it was my duty to purge every error encountered at the time it was met, but "redeeming the time" is a much better way. We should strive to win confidence and build the kind of ground work that will cause the individual to not be offended when error is pointed out, but rather to accept it. "Redeeming the time" is a phrase that would be wonderful to see practiced more. Another Scripture that might help to teach us how to redeem the time is Matthew 10:16: "Behold, I send you forth as sheep in the midst of wolves; be ye therefore wise as serpents, and harmless as doves." No servant of the Lord should be harmful to the cause of Christ, even if the individual does not accept the truth, therefore let us learn the movement of serpents and doves in their work.

The personal evangelist should keep himself out of the way. Jesus said in Matthew 16:24, "If any man will come after me, let him deny himself and take up his cross, and follow me." We should forget our own interests. Peter denied the Lord, trying to forget Jesus and think of his own safety. The Christian thinks of himself and his own presentation and many times forgets the true effort to be put forth. A man was visiting in a neighboring congregation and was called upon to lead the public prayer. After the prayer and sermon, he asked the preacher how he sounded—and was it all right. The preacher had a ready and right answer for him. He said "It does not make any difference how it sounded if the heart was right." You see, he was not denying himself, but thinking of getting himself in the way of his prayer to God for the benefit of sounding good. We should say with Paul, "I am crucified with Christ; nevertheless I live; yet not I, but Christ liveth in me." (Galatians 2:20) Let all who talk to others about Christ get themselves out of the way first. We get our-

selves in the way with our own temper many times, when
we strive to just win an argument and not watch the main
track and the guiding of the precious soul. We become
side-tracked because of our rise and fall of temper. II
Timothy 2:23 says, "But foolish and unlearned questions
avoid, knowing that they do gender strifes." Again, Titus
3:9 says the same thing thusly: "But avoid foolish questions, and genealogies, and contentions and strivings about
the law; for they are unprofitable and vain." The same
should be true of us causing the strife. God's word is to
be presented through reasoning. Isaiah 1:18 says "Come
now, and let us reason together." This does not mean that
we should refuse to correct (see II Timothy 3:16-17) but
it does mean that we should watch our temper. We can
and should be guided through prayer prior to and during
the study session.

Personal Preparation—Your Study

**As you have already noted, many of the excuses were
prompted by a lack of knowledge, experience and confidence.**
The young medical intern with a satchel of medical instruments but without experience and training is not wanted
by most people for the doctor at the operating table. There
is no doubt that Christians have the right instrument—
the Word of God—the Bible—but far too many times
through inexperience the improper use of it does more
damage than good. An individual should be just as diligent
toward getting his training in using the Bible as the intern
is in using the medical instruments. In I Timothy 4:13 we
read, "Till I come, give attendance to reading, to exhortation, to doctrine." This is good advice today.

The first subject of study should be the Bible. We can
never be better teachers of the Bible than we are students
of it. A number of Scriptures emphasize our need to study
the Bible. Matthew 11:29; 2 Timothy 2:2, 15; Philippians 1:11; 1 Peter 1:5-8; 2:2; 2 Peter 3:18. God has

commanded in the Great Commission that we teach the gospel to others. How can we teach that which we do not know? Sometimes, we are guilty of infant teachers—that is more zeal than knowledge, and thus little teaching is accomplished. How many souls will be in hell because we were unable to teach them properly after they gave us a hearing, just because we did not understand the Bible? An account was brought to my attention the other day that stated there were many "Roman Catholics" in the church. At first, I was ready to oppose the statement, but after investigating the meaning, perhaps I should let it stand. The idea expressed was that many in the church are no better taught of the Bible than the Roman Catholics who are encouraged to let the priest interpret for them. "My preacher can tell you" is the equivalent of "I'll ask my priest." Every Christian should have the ability to tell others the reason for the hope that they have and not have to rely upon the knowledge of others. It is not wrong to get help, but if we will study, we will not always have to get help on the same problem. Too many times, we are as Paul said in 1 Timothy 1:7, "Desiring to be teachers of the law; understanding neither what they say, nor whereof they affirm." Let us not be blind teachers for both the teacher and the student will fall into the ditch—Matthew 15:14. People usually believe what comes from authoritative sources. We must let the people see that authority in God's word. An open Bible is a must. Quoting of the Scriptures seems not to accomplish the work; therefore, learn where the Scriptures are and let the prospect read the words for himself. David was familiar with the weapon that he used to defeat Goliath. This weapon was not thrust into his hand upon that occasion for the first time, but he had become skillful with practice prior to that. Christians need to become acquainted with the sword of the Spirit—the word of God. 2 Corinthians 10:3 reads, "For though we walk

in the flesh, we do not war after the flesh (for the wea-
pons of our warfare are not carnal . . .)" and in Ephesians
6:12 we read, "For we wrestle not against flesh and blood,
but against principalities, against powers, against the rul-
ers of the darkness of this world, against spiritual wickedness in high places" . . . the armor that follows is: truth
—righteousness—the gospel—faith—salvation—sword of
the Spirit—word of God.

**The second subject of study should be that of the pros-
pect's beliefs.** To know what the person believes is not a
must, but it certainly does help. Then, if you can familiarize yourself somewhat with the things he believes, you
will be prepared to show where they differ from the Bible. To know the reasons that caused him to have those
beliefs also helps. Was it tradition? Was it through
marriage? Was it through sickness? In knowing these,
several things are accomplished. It allows the worker to
know which way to guide the individual, the problems that
need to be answered, and which ones to answer first. It
also takes the wind out of their sails, so to speak, and
makes the teaching situation much easier. In order to
do this, we constantly must be on our watch to bring out
things new and old. Read in Matthew 13:52: "Then said
he unto them, 'Therefore every scribe which is instruct-
ed unto the kingdom of heaven is like unto a man that is
a householder, which bringeth forth out of his treasure
things new and old." If we know the beliefs, we might
do well to study books of literature from authors acknowledging that belief. A number of books listing the
beliefs of others in an easily understood manner is given
in the Bibliography of this book. Many times the individual does not know what he (or the religious group)
actually believes, even though he holds to it. If we are
aware of those things, then we can guide him and show
him what tenants he holds to in ignorance and should he
be put to the test, would not want to hold to such things

if he really knew that they were as they are. **You need to learn the logic of the Scriptures as well as the illogic of the other's thoughts or beliefs.** An individual might convince himself that he is tired or hungry and think he needs rest or food, but actually not be tired or hungry. We must recognize the truth and cause the prospect to recognize the truth also—rather than the seemingly logic and the conclusions of believing what they want to believe. Can you understand why the public believes that George Washington was the first president? You might answer, "They have been taught to believe that and nothing else." Did you know some writers acknowledge Samuel Green to be the first president, even though he did the work only a few weeks? Checking the evidence or facts will reveal the truth of the matter. Understanding what makes another believe as he does and what it takes to cause him to see just the Bible is important. Many times repetition is the key to the problem—to help people to see the only true church and the only true baptism have enough scriptural references and show them again and again. **Another consideration when studying with an individual is personalities.** It should not be above the Christian to change an aspect of his personality, when it does not involve sin. Paul did. Read 1 Corinthians 9:22: "To the weak became I as weak, that I might gain the weak; I am made all things to all men, that I might by all means save some." If the Christian realizes that he is not the man to study with a particular individual, he should not leave the task undone, but call in another whose personality will work. Remember, we do not convert them to a personal discipleship, but to Christ. Do not be afraid to admit your short-comings in this matter.

The third subject of study should be the individual himself. This sometimes is called "human nature." When we mention this, many shun away, thinking this comes out of a psychology book, but wait; we should learn what

the Bible says about why men hate truth and turn away
from it. John 3:19-21. We need to learn why a man is
fickle. Acts 4:18-19. We need to learn how cowardice
works. John 9:22; 12:42-43. We need to learn how hatred
is demonstrated. John 15:18-27; 7:7. Note how Jesus
deals with a moral man. John 3. We need to learn how
man tries to justify himself. The rich young ruler tried
to justify himself by saying, "All of these things have I
kept from my youth up." We need to learn how to tell
an individual that is fine but not enough, thus wrong.

**Practicing what we have learned is a very important
feature of becoming a successful soul-winner.** It is better
to start and make some mistakes than it is to make the
big mistake of not trying at all. It is recommended that
the personal worker choose individuals that are most apt
to obey early in their personal work, to build up confidence. By individuals "most apt to obey" we mean people who have been attending services for some time and
who have a kind attitude toward discussing Scriptures.
The worker has the responsibility to overcome fear, self-
consciousness, "too proud to do this work" attitude, indifference, self-limitations, ignorance and personality problems. Sometimes we need to develop a mind that is willing to change, if need be, to be more effective. Sometimes we are like the first farmers in America. They
plowed the field by hand, planted it by hand, and reaped
it by hand. We would think it strange in these times if
the farmer were so old-fashioned that he could not see
the need for a change to be productive. If a young lady
desires to gain employment and discovers that she cannot type fast enough with her present hunt and peck
method, she decides to change to a more efficient touch
system. We should likewise be willing to change our experiences as we find that they are not doing the work.
We can never compromise or change the Scriptures or
their meaning one iota, but if there is anything we can

change about ourselves to prepare us to be more effective workers in the Lord's vineyard, we should certainly change it. Of course if we are succeeding, fine. Preachers that stay a few years at a place and convert two or three need to revamp their training and experiences. We have to spend the TIME TEACHING but that must be done in the RIGHT MANNER. Experience is the best teacher only if it is the right teacher. We will make no progress if we fail to practice and still no progress if we do not know how. In the school system, there is a practice-teaching course, where one experienced helps the inexperienced. The same could work very well in this work. The Lord sent them out two by two. We would not be without example. Practice and study causes confidence. The most productive in any area of work are the experienced. Those who advertise for help in the want-ads and who want the most productive say "EXPERIENCED ONLY APPLY." However, we will never become experienced in this work if we do not begin.

Study and goals usually travel together. When in school, the individual studies with a definite aim or goal in mind. Many would not continue their studies if they thought there were no end, no reward, no pleasure. When we study for the great work of soul-winning we can visualize the salvation of the souls of men and women—even our own. This causes us to prepare harder. Then when we are actually in the study situation, we work toward that same goal. Too often, Christians do not know what they can accomplish because they work in a hit and miss fashion. We should not be afraid to establish goals and strive to fulfill them. Numbers are not contrary to God's law, because there is a soul behind every number. The Lord spoke to one in some accounts, and he spoke to 5,000 in an audience that he fed with fish and bread. We should be interested in every soul in the world, yet be able to confine our immediate interest in one individual soul when we prepare to study with him. Beginning goals should not be too high. One soul a year is more than none and more than many are bringing into the fold now. Of course, the minimum goal could and should be increased from time to time with greater experience. Speaking of goals, we should accomplish certain things with the prospect; that is, individual goals to accomplish the overall goal, such as gaining the appointment, causing the prospect to listen and understand and causing the individual to act. Goals are used in salesmanship. We are personal workers showing Jesus Christ and a way of salvation—not merchandise but teaching Christ and His way. A preacher one time told me he was not selling anything—that it was a gift. We agree with that conclusion, but don't you think we have to persuade as Paul did when he encouraged others to become Christians? Persuasion—whether an exchange of material objects or a way is selling or convincing people of the right way. In salesmanship, if a person makes ten contacts and averages three sales, it behooves the salesperson to make thirty contacts to make nine sales. It proves the same in teaching others. If an individual wants to convert one a month—he should contact one each week. If he wants to convert two a year, he will have to contact eight a year. Yes, we should set a goal and strive to fulfill it. The little motto that so many used in 1951 would be a good starter but should not be the end: "Each One Win One." Now for an important transition point: Do not just think in terms of numbers, but do think in terms of a precious soul—remember that the church is made of souls saved **One by One.**

GETTING THE APPOINTMENT

The Ground Work

Getting the appointment is sometimes called the approach or groundwork. It also may be termed "getting the interview or arousing interest." Recently one of the elders here went with me to study with a lady. After the study was over, I asked him to give me his first impression. He said "I was amazed to know that she was ready to study and didn't think it was possible to prepare people to be ready to open the Bible and study so easily." Of course, much work had already been accomplished prior to this appoinmtent. Getting the person ready to accept the study of the Bible for what she would honestly read for herself was more than one-half of the battle. If we do not get near the prospect, no matter how well we know our Bible, we will not show him the knowledge he needs to know. At least 50% of the effectiveness of any conversion is due to the proper laying of the ground work.

We should learn to present one thing at a time while trying to gain the appointment as well as during the actual study. Many times the individual is popping so many questions that he not only confuses you but is actually confused himself. A person called on the telephone and asked a question about instruments of music. Before that question could be answered, another had been received, and before that one was answered, still another had been asked. He was honestly searching, but was confusing himself and me as well, without intending to do so. He would have been better off presenting one problem at a time and solving it accordingly. We must learn to solve one problem at a time. A woman who allows one item of clothing at a time to go through the washing machine wringer is more apt to complete the washing than the woman who puts too much through at a time—her wringer will become clogged. Often, if we are asking questions, it is best to postpone an answer and arrange an appointment so that things may be handled in the right order and at the right time. If you are trying to make an appointment, it is better to choose one or two well chosen thoughts and present them accordingly, arousing interest.

Value of Definite Appointments

Should we make definite appointments in the Lord's work or should we use a hit and miss method and hope we have an appointment? Many salespersons go from door to door, trying to interest people in an article without any prior preparation. Statistics show the rate of sales in such approaches to be very low. Similarly, in arranging periods of Bible study, if you know something of the individual's character and teachings, you can better help him to study the Bible. It helps you in your presentation of the gospel truths. Also, if the individual knows you are coming, there is less chance for antagonism and his heart is better prepared to receive the truth presented. There are exceptions to this rule. Sometimes the appointment should be made with the husband or wife, mother or loved one and as much of the ground work as is possible laid from that angle and then the approach made and a study begun in a very impromptu manner. Let us look at such a situation. I recall a man in California who was not a member of the church. His wife was very faithful. It seemed there was no way to cause this individual to want to discuss the Bible. An appointment was made with the wife and we promised to be there at a definite time. She managed to have supper over, dishes done and no excuses in the way to prevent or hinder my broaching the subject. We arrived at their home to find them in the front room, visiting with each other. To my surprise, and not knowing to this date whether she planned it or not, the lady was called by a neighbor to her house. Imagine being alone with her husband and he had no idea when his wife would come back. We talked about a number of things that interested him. Then, he did not want to be rude and changed the subject from him to a more general item. I knew less about this and just remained silent for awhile. Then he did not introduce another subject. Silence was what was needed. I asked in a low, humble, sincere voice, "Have you ever thought about where you will spend eternity?" He confided in me that honestly he had, but no one had ever talked to him about it. We proceeded with the conversation and soon he asked several questions. I asked him if he minded if I went to the car to get my Bible (You should always keep your Bible nearby). Even though the appointment was not with the husband, definite ground work had been laid. His wife returned just as the study began, and after several hours of diligent study, the man told me he would like to obey the gospel that evening. Indefinite appointments are usually not the best. Should an opportunity arise during a casual visit, it is usually best to book a definite appointment for a later study, simply because the rapport is not properly set up. If they are not set in mind as to the reason for your coming, then they will at least have that opportunity before the time for the actual study appointment rolls around. This also tends to cause an argumentative person to do less arguing.

Getting the attention is a must. This means undivided attention. How does a teacher in the school system get attention in her classroom? She calls for it. Often Bible school teachers need to learn this lesson—also some preachers. It is equally true in the private study period. Getting attention means asking for it and holding it so that it is undivided. The Christian cannot use the bazaars, entertainment and false fronts, but we must use only the Bible. It is amazing how many wives who are contending that they are Christians have never called for their husband's attention to study the Bible with them. No doubt many have talked religion with them and ended up in arguments, rather than actually opening the Bible. There are others who are afraid they will force them or make them angry. To live in such fear should have been considered prior to marriage. Getting the attention wasn't hard prior to marriage, at least they were asked to marry. Getting the attention for their soul's salvation is more important than getting their attention to the preacher to say "I do." The open Bible is the best attention holder in relationship to the destiny of man. A Bible from which quotations are given usually provokes arguments. An open Bible, allowing the individual to read the truths for himself, will hold attention, especially if the individual has never seen the truths before.

Unexpected things often gain attention. (1) When the individual is expecting you to argue and you do not, the unexpected lack of argument gains attention. Unexpected agreement causes the person to be interested in you personally and to listen. We need to agree wherever truth is found. Certainly, never agree with error, even if it comes from the best of a friend. Agree where you can and you have gained attention. You will note in the section on Scriptures, that those Scriptures that are basic and most apt to be agreed upon are placed first. This lays a groundwork for the time when the prospect is not apt to accept certain teachings later in the study. (2) If you know something of what the prospect proposes to believe, although you do not have to, you have gained his attention. (3) Unexpected questions usually gain attention. Remember always ask them so as to get a "Yes" or a positive "No." Several of these might be: "Wouldn't it be wonderful if there were only one church today?" or "Wouldn't it be wonderful if the world were united religiously?" or "Isn't it a shame that there are so many churches?" or "I've been praying about your spiritual status a long time—have you?" (4) We gain their attention and hold it by the way we answer their questions: "I've never been baptized, am I saved?" would be answered well if we reply, "Now it wouldn't make much difference what I said about that, would it? Would you like to see what Jesus said concerning it?" (5) Gain their attention by rebuilding confidence over ill-will. Often we hear, "I do not want to belong to that church because they teach that you are going straight to hell if you are not baptized (or for some other conclusion)." Unfortunately, someone has laid the wrong kind of ground work. Of course, do not apologize for the truth stated in such a conclusion. The aim is to gain attention (I might say that you have it in a sense but it is negative) so as to cause the individual to see that conclusion is in the Bible and accept it as the truth. A direct question would help here, simply, "Would you like to see what the Bible teaches concerning that subject?" Note this does not commit yourself right then as to the answer but does cause the individual to be prepared to receive the God given answer—whether it agrees with him or not. (6) Often we gain their attention by an unexpected manner of handling age-old excuses, such as: "I'm just as good as the fellow who attends church all of the time" and "My mother's church is good enough for me." Ask the individual if he will study with you and show you in the Bible the Scriptures backing up such statements. If he admits he could not find them, say "May we study them together? Your mother was a religious person and I'm sure she would want you to study the Bible, wouldn't she?" (7) If the individual asks you a direct question that would only provoke argument if answered right then, such as "What authority do you have for not using mechanical instruments of music in the worship?" gain his attention by offering the unexpected, that is, offer to take some of your time to come to his home and show him the answer to this question right out of the Bible. Always strive to gain an appointment rather than answer questions on the spur of the moment. This will allow you to study more problems, rather than just that immediate one. Jesus taught us this point by pointing out to the disciples, especially in the gospel of Mark, that they should "Go and tell no man" often. This did not mean that He wanted them to postpone an answer forever, but rather tell the world that Jesus was the Christ, the Son of the Living God when the time was ready. Colossians 4:5 also brings out this same thought: "Walk in wisdom toward them that are without, **redeeming the time.**" If we answer spontaneously, argument usually follows. Be on the alert to turn most interested statements into an appointment.

Usually it is wise to have a definite time ready to offer when you can give the appointment. Try to decide upon one day a week for your study appointments. You can remember the filling of one day easier than you can remember seven days, and then save that day each week for study periods. If an individual cannot make this day or evening, then tell him you will check for another day and confirm it, if it is suitable with him. One of the hardest things for the beginner in this work is to make the definite appointment. One individual told me he had tried and tried and failed. Remember, everyone will not give an appointment, and everyone who studies will not obey the gospel. It was said in the offset of this section that fifty per cent of the success is due to the proper laying of the ground work and usually the main part of the ground work is making the appointment. The door is open when the appointment is made. Practice and even if you fail in making appointments, you will have gained more experience towards the time when you will succeed more and more. Once the appointment is made, be sure to keep it and to be prompt.

Where to Get the Appointments
Where do you begin to look for appointments? A preach-

er once asked me, "Where do you find so many prospects
with whom to study?" Another told me he had baptized
his last two prospects that night. Prospects for appointments are everywhere. There is no need for competition
between individuals nor between congregations in this
field of endeavor. Christians who have spouses that have
not obeyed the gospel are the most likely prospects, because usually they have attended some with their wives
or husbands or have seen literature or listened to their
loved ones tell them of the saving gospel. Every personal worker should make a list of prospects and work them
out systematically. The visitors who attend services are
also good prospects. Those who call you on the telephone
are good prospects, especially those that call to have spiritual help or to ask a Bible question. Those persons getting married are also good people to whom to present the
gospel. Usually it is wise in such a case to make an appointment with the people early in their married life. An
individual that complains about some religious group or
even dislikes some of the things he has seen in members
of the church of Christ gives opportunity to be taught in
a private session. If you are conducting a Bible Correspondence Course, those who complete the course are very
likely prospects. In fact, every individual with whom you
talk gives rise in some way to change the conversation to
a religious subject and make an appointment. Remember, the more appointments a person has, the more results he is most apt to have in conversions, but he must
be sincerely interested in each one and devote time to
study each case separately and to pray about it.

Calling for the appointment is important. We should
make definite appointments, either in person, by writing,
or by calling on the telephone. Do not be afraid to call
someone and bring his attention to the fact that we go into homes and answer individual questions direct from the
Bible and do not be afraid to ask if the person has some

questions he would like answered and if the answer is affirmative, be prepared to set a definite time, such as, "Would Tuesday at 7 o'clock be all right with you?" Make a practice of writing letters if you cannot talk to them personally or by telephone. The following letter is an exact copy of one written from which an appointment was received, the study was conducted, and the lady did obey the gospel on the following Sunday morning:

> "Dear Mrs. _____:
>
> I am sorry that I have not been able to contact you at the services with regard to studying the Bible. I am, therefore, using this means to make a tentative appointment with you for 7:00 p.m., Tuesday, September 27, 1955. Will you please call 5-9967 some morning for confirmation or another definite appointment. If I do not hear from you, I will assume that you are not able to keep this appointment.
>
> Sincerely,"

It is true that some will call you and that you can have appointments to study because that is their motive in calling, however, most appointments have to be prompted by you. There is another method of gaining the appointment that has not been mentioned. That is the "long range" approach. Some persons are antagonistic or need to be won over to your confidence. If a loved one refuses to study the Bible, or is known to be belligerent toward the church, this approach is best. Sometimes friends in the church need to help you by calling upon them and causing them to see their happiness or the fact that they actually are human. Maybe you need to go fishing with them, or hunting, or even invite them to a meal with you. Most of the time, if you study after a meal, it is best to let them know the reasons for bringing them together. If you sneak up on them—using the meal as an excuse— they usually know it and if inclined toward antagonism they will be hurt. Let me make one statement of warning concerning the "long range" approach. Don't let it be so "long range" that nothing definite is ever accomplished. Sometimes a natural visitation can be turned into a study period but you must learn how to do this without the least bit of antagonism. For instance, a suggestion has already been made that the Bible be close, preferably in the car if at their home or in its natural place at your home. If a question is asked, by all means consider the best of two approaches: (1) If the evening is young, and time will permit, begin the study in the right way. (2) If the evening does not afford enough time to do the study justice, then make an appointment to have a definite study at a later time. No less than two hours should be used in a study and usually no more than three at any one sitting.

Bringing the subject around to making an approach is important. In the fourth chapter of John, we see how Jesus turned the conversation of water into the subject "water of life." He proceeded from there to the woman's sins and she desired to change the subject and again Jesus changed the subject to "Worship in spirit and truth." We can change most subjects into a religious vein of thought and accomplish a great deal of work for the Lord. A direct question will also change the subject so that we can make a question for an appointment. Jesus used questions over and over again. There are over 400 recorded questions in the four gospels. A direct question often accomplishes much—even in an evil avenue of approach. Often the criminal begins his evil work by asking a question, "Hey bud, got a match?" We may even ask, "May I change the subject?" The Lord opened the approach with a question by asking "Give me to drink." Recently a man asked me if Masonry were compatible with the Scriptures. I asked him if he would like to have me come to his home to study that subject in light of the Scriptures since the place (grocery store) was not the place and certainly it would take more time than he could afford there to study the subject properly. He consented and we agreed upon a definite time.

Objections are usually made at the time that you try to gain an appointment. Statements are often made on a religious subject that can be turned into an appointment. Some of these have already been noted and this section will deal with some more problems. What would you answer if you were endeavoring to gain an appointment and the problems below were given you? Write out your suggested solutions to see how near you can come toward getting an appointment, then compare the solutions given on the following pages. Use an additional sheet of paper and identify them by number.

APPROACH PROBLEMS	YOUR SOLUTION

1. The man says nothing but demonstrates that he is not interested. His wife is a member of the church.

2. "I'm not interested in changing churches right now."

3. "I've never been baptized, am I saved?"

4. "I'll study with you if you will first tell me why you do not use mechanical instruments of music."

5. "I do not want to belong to that church because they teach that you are going straight to hell if you are not baptized!" (Or some other conclusion).

6. "I'm just as good as the fellow who attends all the time."

7. "My mother's church is good enough for me."

8. "No, sir, I'll not study the Bible with you—I was always taught not to discuss politics and religion!"

9. "I will study with you if you will let me put in my ideas too and say what I want."

10. "I'm afraid I cannot live the Christian life, so I will not try it at all."

11. "I'm not ready to settle down and study it now—maybe later."

12. "I'm already a church member" or "I feel I'm saved already."

13. "Honestly, do you think it makes any difference what we believe as long as we are all striving to go to heaven?"

14. "I am a Catholic and besides we do not use the same Bible."

15. "No, you people believe you are the only ones going to heaven."

16. "I do not believe in the Bible, heaven or hell."

17. "The Bible is full of contradictions, therefore, I am not interested in studying it."

The aim is to get the appointment and not convince the individual on his immediate objection that you are right and he is wrong. The greatest error is to strive to answer the objection when raised and usually this ends up only in arguing. If the conversation should take such a turn that no appointment is secured, honestly review your part of the conversation to see if any answers you made were argumentative or insincere. Some of these solutions may be interchanged. There are no hard and fast answers but a proper attitude will prepare you for a natural, sincere answer rather than a "book" answer. The main thing is to formulate the proper attitude toward gaining appointments. The suggested solution is at the far right in this section.

APPROACH PROBLEMS	SUGGESTED SOLUTIONS:
1. The man says nothing but demonstrates that he is not interested. His wife is a member of the church.	1. Long range approach: Try to gain his confidence by inviting him to dinner or golfing or fishing, etc.
	2. Make arrangements with the wife to be present some evening. Be sure to tell her to let you guide the conversation (She has failed thus far; allow another to try). Let her use her judgment in telling him whether you are coming or not. If she tells him, caution her to tell him in such a manner that he will want to receive your company. By all means do not say, "I've invited someone over who is going to show you where you are wrong."
	3. Opening religious remarks: "Have you ever thought where you will spend eternity?" or "Have you ever thought about your soul's salvation?"
2. "I'm not interested in changing churches right now."	1. "By using the term churches—you recognize the fact that there are too many. Wouldn't it be wonderful if all the religious world were united?" (Aim is to

get "Yes" for an answer) or "Wouldn't it be wonderful if there were only one church today?" (The truth is there is only one approved of God) or "Isn't it a shame that there are so many churches?" (All of these should cause "Yes" answers).

2. "Wouldn't you like to see how we can be united religiously?" or "Wouldn't you like to study the Bible and see how there can be only one church?"

3. "I've never been baptized, am I saved?"

1. "Now it wouldn't make much difference what I said about that, would it?"

2. "Would you like to see what Jesus (or the Bible) says concerning that?"

4. "I'll study with you if you will first tell me why you do not use mechanical instruments of music."

1. The aim is to tell him why but not first.

2. "This is a good question, have you any more?"

3. "May I write this down and come by your house next Tuesday (or any other time you have free—or upon which you can agree) to let the Bible tell you why?"

4. If they insist upon you telling them first, "I promise to answer that after we see what the Bible says concerning some things upon which I feel we can agree."

5. "I do not want to belong to that church because they teach that you are go-

1. Warning: Do not apologize for the truth.

2. "Would you like to see

ing straight to hell if you are not baptized!"
(Or some other conclusion).

6. "I'm just as good as the fellow who attends all of the time."

7. "My mother's church is good enough for me."

8. "No, sir, I'll not study the Bible with you—I was taught not to discuss politics and religion."

what the Bible teaches on that subject?"

3. "Have you ever read that in the Bible?"

1. "Would you like to see what the destiny of such persons is from the Bible?"

2. "Are there any good people in the church that you know who you would like to imitate?"

3. "What Scriptures approve of your present activities?" (Pick up one of the other solutions that will fit his answer).

1. "If I come to your home next Tuesday will you show me what Scriptures teach about her church?"

2. If he does not know where they are: "May I come over and help you hunt for them?"

3. "Your mother was a religious person, wasn't she?" This wins confidence and should cause him to want to read his Bible as the mother did, implied by his excuse.

1. Long range approach: Try to gain his confidence by inviting him to dinner or golfing or fishing, etc.

2. Assume that you may have hurt him due to his abrupt answer and reply: "I did not mean to hurt you." He may then tell you the reason why, for that is the problem.

3. "May I ask you why you do not want to study the

greatest Book of all?" No doubt one of the other objections will be given—then handle it accordingly.

9. "I will study with you if you will let me put in my ideas too and say what I want."

1. Agree: "I would be happy to have you do that." (This will allow you to see what he believes and upon what things you agree so that you can compliment him on that).

10. "I'm afraid I cannot live the Christian life, so I will not try it at all."

1. This man assumes that it will cost so much without the help of the Lord that he cannot endure. "May we study the Bible and show you how the Lord will help you live the Christian life?"

2. "Would you like to see what the cost is from the Bible?"

3. "Have you ever tried to let the Lord help you live the Christian life?" Pause for answer and then say, "You will never know until you have tried."

4. "Have you ever thought that all you have to give up is just those items that are unscriptural?"

11. "I'm not ready to settle down and study it now—maybe later."

1. "Are you satisfied with your soul as it is now if you should die in this condition?"

2. Assume the "later" is just a short time and agree "That would be better—would (and give a date about two months away) that be all right with you?"

12. "I'm already a church member." or
"I feel I'm saved already."

1. Which church would that be? After you receive the answer, use some of the other approaches given in this section.

2. "If I come to your home next Tuesday, will you give me the Scriptures showing that church to be the one Jesus established?"

3. "Now you are a member of one church and I am a member of another. We are divided, aren't we? May we study to see how we may be united?"

13. "Honestly, do you think it makes any difference what we believe as long as we are all striving to go to heaven?"

1. "May I come over next Tuesday evening and answer that directly from the Bible?"

2. "Would you like to see what the Bible teaches that we should believe?"

3. "Does it make any difference whether we rob a bank or not—whether we murder or not? In like manner, has God revealed anything that does make a difference in living in society and worshipping him? May we study that difference in the Bible?"

14. "I am a Catholic and besides we do not use the same Bible."

1. "I'll be happy to study with you out of the Catholic Bible."

15. "No, you people believe you are the only ones going to heaven."

1. "Do you think it makes any difference what man teaches? May we see what the Bible says about who is going to heaven?"

2. "Will you please show me the Scriptures which grant

a hope to any other religious group?" (Be sure to say in right tone voice).

16. "I do not believe in the Bible, heaven or hell."

1. "Do you believe in night and day? Pause for "yes" answer and then reply: "You believe in some of the Bible for it teaches the same truth." The same reasoning can be given concerning birth and death and a multitude of other truths.

2. "Would you like to believe other things if the Bible says so?" If "Yes" then "May we see what it says?"

3. If utter rejection of the Bible, present some of the information supplied in the chapter entitled "Preparing the individual to accept the Bible as the Word of God."

17. "The Bible is full of contradictions, therefore, I am not interested in studying it."

1. "Please give me one contradiction."

2. Usually they fumble around. When you hear one supposed contradiction, ask, "May I come to your home next Tuesday evening and let us examine the Scriptures to see if this is really a contradiction?"

3. II Peter 3:16 "As also in all his epistles, speaking in them of these things; in which are some things hard to be understood, which they that are unlearned and unstable wrest, as they do also the other Scriptures, unto their own destruction."

METHOD OF ACTUAL STUDY

The Environment

The place of study is very important. Sometimes it is better to study in your home or in the church building or in another's home, instead of the home of the prospect. Certain factors determine this. If the home environment is such that in it the prospect cannot concentrate, then another place should be sought. If the individual has been coming to the services, the building may be in order. Sometimes an individual may invite the personal worker and the prospect to his home for the study. In such a case, it should be emphasized that only the prospect and the person directing the study should do most of the talking.

The atmosphere is important wherever the study is conducted. If the lights or ventilation are not as good as possible, then it affords the prospect an excuse to stop the study anytime. If you let him know that you are endeavoring to eliminate such hindrances, then he will not look for others either. After you have entered the home, or other location of the proposed study, you should talk on several generalities and especially things of interest to him. If you have made an appointment, and most of the time you should have, he expects you to change the subject to the reason for your presence. The personal worker should take the initiative in starting the study, usually within ten to fifteen minutes after entering. This transition may be made by such a statement as this: "May I change the subject to religion?" (maybe adding) "Now you expected me to do this, didn't you?" or you may suggest the environmental problem as your transition point. If you do not, by all means suggest it after the subject is changed. You may say, "Would it be out of order if I suggest that we all study at the kitchen (or dining room) table?" Peo-

ple are very much at home at the table and usually it
offers the proper writing space and area for open Bibles.
If the lights are not proper, you might suggest bringing
in a floor lamp from the living room or even ask them if
they have a brighter bulb. It is always wise to ask the
lady of the house to provide glasses for each and some
water. Here is a good place to suggest the reason for re-
moving possible excuses. You suggest that when people
study you have found that they usually need a drink of
water and also it removes any obstacle that might inter-
rupt the study.

**The persons present also should be considered in light
of the environment.** Of course, those that you desire to
teach should be there, but sometimes there can be too
many of them. Usually it is best to limit it to the man
and wife. If others have been invited and are present,
they should take their places at the table and be told
(kindly) to let the conversation be between the prospect
and the personal worker, unless they are asked a direct
question by the personal worker. If they have questions,
let them ask later. It is hard enough to direct the thoughts
of one person into the proper channels, and it is almost
impossible to direct several minds properly in such a concentrated study as this. Early in my preaching career, I
was invited to a home to study with a family. The arrange-
ments were made to study in the kitchen and shortly after
we began studying the husband's parents arrived and were
seated at the table. Later the wife's parents arrived and
we moved to the living room. Later the preacher of the
denomination to which they belonged arrived, and I polite-
ly invited him to the study. This made seven prospects
and of course I thought (just beginning) that all could be
converted, since all of them appeared eager to study. Later
it was learned that they were invited to arrive that way.
I found that was not the proper way to conduct such a
study because one mind confused another and with so

many questions and statements being made no one was
helped (except I learned that you can have too many prospects). If you know the prospect has children, ask the
prospect about their presence and conduct. If they will
be in bed, or with a baby sitter, fine. If no such arrangement is planned, then you take a baby-sitter along in the
person of your wife, friend, or fellow-laborer. Recently
an elder went with me to study with a lady. He had not
been with me in such a study before and was interested in
the method of study. The woman's children were noisy
and clamored all over her. The elder ended up taking
care of the children, and allowed the prospect to concentrate and apply what she was studying. Many times my
wife has taken the prospect's children to another room
and read books, told stories, even given babies their bottles
and put them to bed, so the people with whom we were
endeavoring to study could clear their minds of physical
needs and only concern themselves in that hour of spiritual
needs.

**The items to be used in the study period should be
arranged prior to entering the home.** Of course, the worker should have prepared the presentation prior to this
time. He should have marked his Bible so as to have a
ready reference to the Scriptures. See the chapter on
Scriptures. He should take along three or four Bibles
with the same pagination, if possible. This way he can
call out the page instead of the Scripture or, better, along
with the Scriptures. Many persons with whom you study
will not know the Scripture locations. This tends to em-
barrass them and slow down the study. If you have several Bibles, alike, then the study will progress nicely. If
you do not have Bibles alike, here again your wife or a
friend can be very helpful. If the prospect cannot easily
find the Scriptures, you can casually suggest your wife or
the friend help him—but always urge the prospect to
read the Scriptures aloud himself. The worker should

also take along a pencil and some paper on which to write notes to leave with the prospect after the study. The personal worker should also have a concordance with him, either in the back of his Bible or he should take with him a separate Cruden's Concordance. If no appointment has been made, it is wiser to leave the books in the car, or, if they have come to your home, have them in their natural place. No little thought should be given to the items necessary in your study. They are not many, and should not cause much trouble, but should be easily mastered. Sometimes the hostess has several items of refreshments to add to the occasion. If she has them prepared, indulge graciously. It is wiser, however, to suggest prior to coming that she not be bothered with refreshments, because it just allows an opportunity to break up the study and many times this is detrimental. They usually jump up at the wrong time. Sometimes when refreshments are offered and you have no other alternative, it is better to postpone the completion of the study to another time. Then, at that time, review (in brief form) the previous study before going into new subjects.

Opening Remarks

By all means, do not plunge into the study with your your first remarks, unless the prospect throws you into such a situation. Of course, confidence should have been won prior to entering the home, but that kind of confidence needs to be furthered now by "getting close" to the prospect. Learn something of his work, former places of residence, interests, children, education, lawn, car, house, hobbies, the weather. Certainly do not discuss all of the listed items in your opening remarks—these are merely for suggestions, but do make it a common conversation of things which concern the prospect, thereby weaving him into your opening remarks. All of this can afford you an opportunity to use illustrations that he will understand when you are presenting God's Word to him. If you know of his work, when you teach on authority, you can make an application in the study. The first remarks should not continue into a conversation so interesting that it overshadows or is prolonged so long that the remembrances of the evening are the interesting things discussed earlier, or so long that there is little time left for the actual study. You must leave the first remarks sometime, therefore, learn how to make the transition to the actual study. Usually some remark will be made that will help you change the subject easily. If not, then just begin with remarks appropriate to the occasion which have already been discussed in this chapter.

Remember the name of your prospect—this is valuable to a study. It may be wise to ask for his first name and for permission to use it (except if the prospect is much older or where the personality might object). This will help you become closer to him and cause him to know you are personally interested in him. Practice remembering names—if you are genuinely interested in someone, you can make yourself remember his name.

The first words of the actual study should be very carefully chosen. After you have been seated at the table (or other place if it cannot be arranged) and after the books are in place and the water on the table, you should tell them that you are entering a serious time—that of considering what God wants man to do. It is wise to ask for permission to have prayer and to word a short prayer. The personal worker needs God's help—he cannot do this alone. 1 Thessalonians 5:17 tells us to "Pray without ceasing" and certainly we must in studying with people. Pray before you go, when you start, and pray silently all the time during the study. It is hard to argue with a man when you have a prayer on your heart for him. One thing that you should remember to ask when you pray aloud at the beginning of a study is guidance to have the Word of God received in the hearts of all present and the courage to do the things they have learned or will learn. With such a beginning, you are ready to embark upon the first Scripture as shown in the chapter entitled "Scriptures."

An Open Bible

A closed Bible is often another way of saying, "I'll quote it to you." Quoting is not an open Bible. Quoting the Scriptures is a wonderful thing and all should be able to do so, but this is one occasion when it will not help. To quote is often to start an argument. A man who is not afraid of the Bible will read it direct. People who are afraid of what it says for fear it will tell them things to do and things to quit doing must be helped to want to investigate it. A man who is afraid to open his Bible because he knows it will condemn him should be afraid. We should not want our way but the Lord's way. Allow it to direct us in His way. The Bible can guide all minds because it contains the way of a Mind Superior to any who live upon this earth. Man should not be embarrassed to be shown wrong, but should have that feeling that he wants to be right with God. No feeling is so good as to feel right and to be able to find a "Thus saith the Lord" for the practices in which you engage.

An open Bible is a must. The Chinese say that one picture is worth more than 10,000 words. Paul stated he would rather speak five words with understanding than 10,000 in an unknown tongue. What pictures do we have to show? With what understanding can we present them? Even though we use words to show our pictures, we can in the Bible truly paint the picture of Christ and His teachings, the way of unity with Christ and His followers, and the picture of those things that are sinful and harmful to our souls. To allow the prospect to read the words off the printed page is much more effective than to quote or talk about them. The prospect's interest is in what the Bible

says—not in how much you can quote. Often remarks
such as "I've never seen that before" or "Why hasn't someone shown that to me?" have been made. One time when
we were reading I Timothy 2:5, which tells us there is
"one" mediator and that mediator is Jesus Christ, a man
who believed there were others stated, "it looks like that
one is not Mary." He could see it and was honest to take
the truth revealed. Of course, there are those who will
not accept it when shown, but that is a truism about which
Christ told us. It may be like a man that is untrained in
the works of art entering an art museum. He just doesn't
see anything beautiful or interesting. If the proper ground
work had been laid before entering the museum, he would
have appreciated it. So we must be careful in the work
that goes on before entering the beautiful art galleries of
the Bible.

God commands and teaches us to search the Scriptures.
John 5:39 tells us "Search the Scriptures, for in them ye
think ye have eternal life; and they are they which testify
of me." It is the Scriptures from which we desire to know
the lessons. Sometimes, men want to examine everything
under the sun prior to finding what the Bible says. Some
people in searching for the truth search in the various
churches, but this is the wrong method. We should search
the Bible rather than the churches: search the Bible and
the right church will be found. Suppose you have a fountain pen and someone tells you it is gold. If you should desire to really know, you would not ask for my fountain pen
and examine it—that which is in question is your fountain
pen and we must examine that one. That which is in question in religion is the Bible and it should always be examined. Hebrews 5:9 states, "And being made perfect, He
became the author of eternal salvation unto all them that
obey Him." Yes, we should search the Author's work
which contains the way of eternal life. Philip knew this
lesson well for in Acts 8:35 we read, "Then Philip opened

his mouth and **began at the same Scripture** and preached unto him Jesus." Our beginning, continuing and ending should be from the Scriptures. Many times the reason we fail is because we think something else will work better than the Scriptures. If we will let the prospect read from the Bible, he will see that it is powerful. See Romans 1:16. Using the Bible eliminates arguments because the prospect can see it is God's Word—not yours. An individual needs to see the Scriptures in black and white for himself in order to be able to apply them to his own life. A few years ago, we were studying with a Catholic friend. He read in Matthew 28:18-20 that "all authority" had been given to Christ, "in heaven and on earth" and of course this left no authority to be given to the pope who is upon the earth. Immediately he remarked, "The fathers never showed us this Scripture." He could see the truth for himself and it did not take a long discourse to preach Jesus. He was 66 years of age and was baptized the following Sunday. He was converted as the Ethiopian eunuch because the Scriptures accomplished what they were given to do. Isaiah 55:11 tells us "My word shall not return to me void." In salesmanship, the salespeople learn that more sales are made by samples than any other type of selling. It is, therefore, wise to put the Bible in the prospect's hands, let him see it by reading its message. Show him how wonderful it is that we can support our beliefs and practices on the message of Christ. Remember a carpenter is inefficient if he does not have his tools, or if he misuses them, even so, a servant of the Lord will be just as inefficient without his Bible or if he misuses it. Many sales organizations have installed mirrors in the showrooms so that the prospective buyer may see himself in the merchandise. This refers especially to clothes, automobiles and jewelry. If we can allow the individual to see himself and the Bible together, he usually can see its application. Many denominationalists have not allowed the people to

see what is wrong in their religion. The reason many do
not see the Bible alike is because of a failure to examine
it. We talk about it, quote from it and talk around it, yet
fail to cause others to see what God actually revealed in
it. Since these methods have failed, let us make a plea to
begin the practice of opening our Bible and more and more
people will see it just as it was written.

Procedure

**Cause the individual to read aloud the Scriptures to
be discussed.** This will help in a number of ways. It will
tell you, as the personal worker, to be sure the prospect is
reading the Scripture that will answer the problem at
hand. After more experience, it will permit you a little
freedom to concentrate and think of the Scriptures and
presentation that should follow. It will help the prospect
reason from error to truth. It will also be the proof of the
pudding, telling you whether the individual is intent on
actually studying with the right attitude. If he does not
want to read the Scriptures, he will probably try to deviate
from them greatly, thus changing the subject or desiring
to argue. If he sees that you are serious in presenting the
lessons of Christ rather than the lessons of men which he
might prefer, he will sometimes try to not read, even after
the appointment is made. An appointment was made one
time with a man who was a member of the Church of the
Brethren. After entering the home and discussing general subjects, the conversation was changed to the Bible.
When he discovered that I handed him a Bible from which
to read, he tried to direct the discussion toward a presentation of his doctrine. I asked him to read the Scriptures to
me from the Bible that backed up what he was saying. He
then told me he could not read without his glasses and
that they were broken last week. Lying on the table nearby was a pair of glasses, and I very casually asked if that
might be an old pair he could use. With hesitation, he

picked them up and said, "Yes" and placed them over his eyes. A Scripture was given, he fumbled and fumbled, then I helped him find it. He saw that I was pressing him to read, and even when the Scripture was found, he said he did not read very well and asked me to read it to him. The man lived alone and evidence in the room led me to believe he read other things—newspapers, magazines and several books were in plain sight. It was evident he actually did not want to study. This illustration is given to show there are a few examples where people will make an appointment and then actually not want to study, but there are so many hundreds of examples where people are willing to study and no attempt has been made to gain an appointment. Causing people to read the Bible aloud is just another effort to remove argumentation and to cause them to actually see the Scriptures for themselves. Far too many people have listened to what their parents have said for years, or their preacher. This is blind acceptance of something religious which usually is not based upon the Scriptures. Many remark, when they actually study it themselves, that they are learning what God wants them to do for the first time in their lives. Having the prospect read aloud will help to remove prejudice because he knows that you as the personal worker did not write what he is reading for himself. Of course, there may be cases where the worker should read the Bible for the prospect, but this is the exception rather than the rule. Most people can read the newspaper and if they can read that, then they can read the Bible. By all means, help to pronounce words in a kind, patient way so that they will get the thought expressed in the message and so they will not be embarrassed. There are some who actually cannot read, and of course read to them. Also, you should read to the sick or the blind without hesitation. In the case of the sick, the length of study should be governed by the nature of the illness. In the case of the blind, it is good to procure the

type of Bible they can read, such as "Moon" or "Braille"—
most State libraries have them to loan. Of course, if they
can read neither, then please do read to them.

**Be sure to advise the prospect that you want to answer
any questions he might have.** When you finish a reading
of all the Scriptures related to each subject, such as
whether we go to the Old Law or the New Law, what
baptism is for and how it is accomplished, stop and ask,
"Do you understand this" or "Do you have any questions
thus far?" If they have questions, then it is best to review, asking them where they are in doubt. Do not proceed until they understand each subject as you present it
from the Bible. At the same time it is usually wise to ask
if they are enjoying the study of the Bible in this manner.
It is easy to ask these questions between subjects, since
the Scriptures are grouped together on one subject to
study before going to another subject. It gains good will
because you are in agreement before going to another subject. Then, if we can cause the individual to say yes, yes,
over and over again, and especially from the beginning
and without argument, then he will be more apt to still
be saying yes at the close of the study and obey what
he has learned. Since the Scriptures are so arranged as
to start where you are most apt to agree, it is wise to
always start with the same Scripture, regardless of the
religion of the prospect. An exception to this rule is
the individual that does not accept the Bible as the
Word of God. In such a case, read the chapter entitled
"Preparing the Individual to Accept the Bible as the
Word of God" and use that chapter. If the prospect tells
of his own plan of salvation, be sure to point out where he
is wrong, using the Scriptures. Should the individual ask
a question that is arranged to be studied later, it is wise
to postpone an answer until that time. If, for instance, at
the very outset the individual asks you to show him Scriptures on why we should not use instruments of music, ask

for his permission to write that question down, state it is a good question, and give your promise that you will answer it a little later, then draw his attention to the subject now at hand. The idea is to answer the question, but at the right time and after the proper ground work has been made. We do not plant seed in the soil until it has been prepared. Causing the individual to begin where you can agree and having him say yes so many times will better prepare him to accept the truth. Let me illustrate: most persons can see the need for having only the fruit of the vine and unleavened bread on the Lord's Table. If they have said yes to this (and other serious subjects) prior to a discussion of the music problem, then you can refer to what they had seen on the Lord's Supper as they read it in the Bible. Yes, by all means answer their questions but do not answer them out of order because it usually provokes argument or premature breaking up of the study, simply because the heart is not fertile enough to receive the seed which is the word of God.

Learn how to use illustrations in your study. The best illustrations are those that come from everyday life. Learn to make practical personal applications of illustrations. It is also very good to use those illustrations you can take from the life of the prospect. Sometimes these illustrations have to be developed as you go along. Sometimes near the end of the study, when you want to point out that Jesus wants us to obey what He has said, meaning what He said and having said what He meant, turn to James 4:17, "To him that knoweth to do good, and doeth it not, to him it is sin." Then in developing the illustration, you can turn to the prospect and ask who is his employer. Finding that out, then imagine some instruction that employer might give, then draw the conclusion of obeying or disobeying that instruction. Usually the point is clearly received. Jesus used things with which the people were familiar in His illustrations of the pearl of great price, the sower, the talents, a mustard seed. He used the simple grass, eating and drinking, and the day itself in Matthew 6:30-34. He took a fact in history for an illustration when he said in Luke 17:32, "Remember Lot's wife." Do not hesitate to fit illustrations into your study as noted, but do be sure they are used properly.

Learn how to use comparison in your study. Comparison may use many illustrations. So many things the prospect may know are right and will not deny can be applied to the proper use of the Scriptures. Jesus likened many things to others to use comparison. In Matthew 13 he used a parable which was an illustration to make his comparison, "The kingdom of heaven is likened unto a man which sowed good seed in his field" and again, "The kingdom of heaven is like to a grain of mustard seed which a man took, and sowed in his field" and again, "The kingdom of heaven is like unto leaven, which a woman took, and hid in three measures of meal." Over and over again, comparison was used by the Master Teacher, Jesus. We can hope to imitate Jesus and use comparison to teach our point. Many times we can take the unknown and show what is likened to that which is known. Always begin with the known. The following chart will demonstrate what we should try to do whether we use illustration, comparison or repetition. There are still other avenues but these are the three most important in personal work.

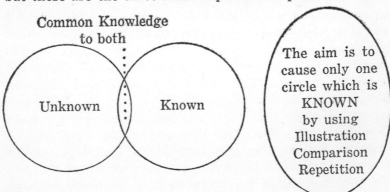

Common Knowledge
to both

Unknown   Known

The aim is to cause only one circle which is KNOWN by using Illustration Comparison Repetition

Learn how to use repetition in your study. Repetition is one of the avenues of learning that is often overlooked. Repetition helps us to remember. Jesus used this type of teaching when He said in the sermon on the mount, "Ye have heard that it was said by them of old time, 'Thou shalt not kill'." He drew their attention to this repetition in their past lives to reveal the lessons of the coming kingdom (church). Again he said "Ye have heard that it was said by them of old time, 'Thou shalt not commit adultery' " and "Ye have heard that it hath been said 'Thou shalt love thy neighbor and hate thine enemy'." Read these verses and others in Matthew 5. In Matthew 19 he used the repetition of their previous teachings to show them the lesson "Have ye not read, that he which made them at the beginning made them male and female . . . " Yes, refer often to the previous lessons they have read and learned and which might be the same principle as that under consideration when they may not understand it or cannot say "Yes." In II Peter 1:12 we read, "Wherefore I will not be negligent to put you always in remembrance of these things, though ye know them, and be established in the present truth." If Peter thought it necessary to constantly refresh minds in that day, bringing again to their remembrance things previously learned, then we too should think it necessary today. Forgetting is easy and a kind remembrance is helpful. Remember, it is charged that most men forget anniversaries and birthdays. A little repetition in remembering will help them to not forget. Repetition is a must in almost every avenue of life. Many times, forgetting a previous thought or action or thing needs to be left forgotten. During World War II, many of the boys remarked that they would never eat Spam once they got back to America. Many of them who said it eat it today and it is a regular selling item on the grocery shelf today. A lady in Washington, D. C., once said that she would never attend the church of Christ again as a result of a

certain sermon. She did not attend for three weeks and on
the day she did return, she obeyed the gospel. Let us
help people remember some things, and leave others forgotten. When I was in school, one of the professors said
that the success of memory was "repetition, repetition,
repetition." Simple answer, but it certainly is true.

SOME DON'TS

Everywhere we hear some DON'TS. In the close relationship of saints with their Creator, as in the close relationship of marriage, there are DON'TS. Some object to
having DON'TS connected with religion, but they should
be there, nonetheless.

1. DON'T be abrupt in your presentation of the study.

2. DON'T be afraid—God is with you.

3. DON'T be rigid but do be NATURAL.

4. DON'T be professional but do be PERSONAL.

5. DON'T represent a religious school or just another
   church among many. Teach Christ and His way.

6. DON'T be afraid to say "I do not know." Should
   you find yourself not knowing the Scriptures re-
   quested on a subject, acknowledge the fact you do
   not know them—don't become confused. Search for
   them then and there if possible and practical; if
   not, make a later appointment to answer that question.

7. DON'T lose interest, and do not conduct yourself so
   that the prospect feels you have lost interest.

8. DON'T seem superior because you feel you are
   right but do guide in a definite way.

9. DON'T be unfriendly. Abraham Lincoln said, "If
   you would win a man to your cause, first convince
   him that you are a sincere friend."

10. DON'T be dogmatic but rather reason as Isaiah
    1:18 encourages. Truth is unchangeable, and our
    attitude should be firm but gentle. Paul said in

1 Thessalonians 2:7: "But we were gentle among you, even as a nurse cherisheth her children."

11. DON'T apologize for the truth—just present it. Read Romans 1:16. Paul was not ashamed of it but realized his responsibility to present it.

12. DON'T compromise the truth as revealed for that would condemn our souls and not save theirs either. Read Galatians 1:6-8.

13. DON'T push people but do PERSUADE them.

14. DON'T tell the individual he will be cast into hell. Let the Bible tell him such information as that and also the other extreme, that Jesus loves all mankind "not wishing that any should perish, but that all should come to repentance" (II Peter 3:9).

15. DON'T refuse to point out error using the Scriptures. 2 Timothy 3:16; 4:2 are clear on this point. Some refuse to point out error saying salespersons do not beat down their competitors—only pointing out the good points. The cause of Christ is not in competition with error. There is only one way to heaven and the Lord revealed that clearly. He Himself reproved and rebuked for our example. In salesmanship, the running down on the needed object is usually done prior to calling in the salesperson. Automobile salespersons are told "DON'T kick their cars" in order to sell. Remember this, the person usually has kicked the car himself or he would not be interested in a new car. In religion it is different—they have not even considered it—it is not a matter of having a new religion but of being right or wrong. Using the automobile illustration again, it is true a car has some points better than others and salespersons can sell some cars without "running down" others but remember all cars do essentially the same thing while all plans of salvation do not. Jesus did not allow the rich young ruler to think all that he had accomplished was sufficient. Jesus did not let Nicodemus think his morality would save him. Jesus said, "Except a man be born again, he cannot see the Kingdom of God." John 3:3. This is the same as saying: your self-righteousness is not sufficient to

save you—you fall short—you have disobeyed—this you need to do because you have not done it yet. Just doing good things will not make one a Christian. A horse does many good things, but that does not make it a Christian.

16. DON'T become angry or lose your self-control. Study Proverbs 25:11; 2 Timothy 2:24-25; James 1:20.

17. DON'T allow the MAIN-TRACK to be SIDE-TRACKED permanently. A train that is side-tracked must get back on the main-track in order to complete the journey. Often we are side-tracked by honest questions. For instance, the prospect may want to know where you can read about the church of Christ in the beginning of the study. It is best to delay until you can show him what the church is. Jesus refused to be kept on the side-track very long by returning to another religious subject in John 4, even though He touched a sore spot in the life of the woman at the well of Sychar. He did that on purpose, not accidentally. Jesus continued His subject by saying "we must worship in Spirit and in truth." He finally reached the point that He wanted to get across to her, "I that speak unto thee am He . . ." (that is, the Messiah that can help you in your life of sin). If we stay on the MAIN-TRACK, we will finally reach the point that we desire to get across. A Doctor that makes an incision must continue with the operation until he is able to make the sutures that close the incision. A prolonged side-tracking may leave the wound in the soul open and active. Let us not be guilty of being side-tracked permanently. CONCENTRATION will help in this regard.

18. DON'T refuse to answer the objections and questions but do answer them at the right time and in the right manner.

19. DON'T refuse to help them overcome their excuses. Many persons hide behind erroneous thinking and religion. We need to help them expose the error of such and see the truth. Having overcome some of our excuses in becoming a personal worker, we should be well equipped to help them overcome some of their excuses.

20. DON'T appear belligerent or smarter than the prospect. Be humble and thankful that God has made it clear to you and that you have the present opportunity in which to teach His will.

21. DON'T talk over the prospect's head. If we have an open Bible, the reading of it will do most of the work and thus we will know where to direct its messages. Abraham Lincoln said, "Don't shoot too high. Aim low enough that the common people will understand."

22. DON'T make it easy for the individual to say "No." Shoe salesmen learn quickly to never ask, "You don't want this pair of shoes, do you?"

23. DON'T enter the study unprepared in subject matter, understanding human nature, and manner of presentation. Be prepared in your heart. Pray before and during the study. Some of these prayers will of necessity have to be silent and private.

24. DON'T let the person think that he is right when he is wrong. This must be done in an appealing tone of voice based upon the intelligence revealed in God's word.

25. DON'T apologize for making him cry if you can or have. People ought to cry more and more over their errors and transgressions. But remember, obedience comes from an intellectual acceptance of the gospel rather than emotional.

26. DON'T let the person forget what he has learned from before. Use repetition to accomplish this.

27. DON'T be smug but be sincerely interested.

28. DON'T be inconsistent but be logical in every thought in which you guide them.

29. DON'T be resentful but try to understand why he thinks the way he does.

30. DON'T judge but let the word judge him as well as his own actions. Remember this lesson and cause the prospect to learn it too. If a lady visits the Doctor and the Doctor tells her she has tuberculosis, remember she had it before the Doctor said

so. His saying so did not make her have it. The Doctor is her friend and not her enemy for telling her so—but he must tell her in a nice way and according to facts. Even so, Christians do not cause the sin of those with whom they study, but they may cause the facts as revealed in the Bible to bring to their attention the sin that has been in the soul long before they were told so. John 5:24, "Verily, verily I say unto you, He that heareth my word, and believeth on him that sent me, hath everlasting life, and shall not come into condemnation, but is passed from death into life." John 12:47-48, "And if any man hear my words, and believe not, I judge him not; for I came not to judge the world, but to save the world. He that rejecteth me, and receiveth not my words, hath one that judgeth him; the word that I have spoken, the same shall judge him in the last day."

31. DON'T be impatient but be patient. God gives the increase, not man. Read 2 Peter 1:5-8; 1 Corinthians 3:6.

32. DON'T have an "I am going to tell you so" attitude but do allow God to tell them as if you were not present.

33. DON'T irritate the individual if you do not get across the Bible teaching. Many people think they have won a battle if they can irritate another, therefore, do not irritate nor allow yourself to become irritated.

34. DON'T give the attitude that you have tripped, trapped or deceived the individual with a method superior to his. We definitely do not want to trap or deceive anyone—we want to persuade more men to study and accept the simple gospel truths. If he refers to your presentation in an attitude to make you feel he thinks he is trapped, tell him you have tried to follow the methods Jesus used and point out that many of these methods are used effectively today by salespersons and are general knowledge and are accessible to all men.

35. DON'T show disappointment if he fails to be baptized. Leave the door open for further instruction if possible.

36. DON'T FAIL TO APPEAL FOR OBEDIENCE OR ACTION. SEE THE CHAPTER ENTITLED "CLOSING."

The Notes to Leave

It is wise to leave the references that you present. You should always write down the Scriptural references and other notes to leave with the prospect—write them down as you go along in the study. Many times the person may feel you are going over the Scriptures faster than he can comprehend them. If you leave the references you remove the attitude that you are going to force the issue on that occasion. You should never "force any issue" at any time. Leaving the Scriptures allows him to honestly study them and to reach a conclusion even if he does not obey at the close of that study period. Leaving notes causes you to be thorough in presenting your lesson. It helps you remember how far you have progressed, should you desire to stop and review or answer a question that is proper at that point. Should you have to make the study into several sessions, it is a guide as to how far you have progressed. Also, a piece of paper before you gives you something to write on to emphasize the Scriptures, to write out charts and illustrations that are shown in the chapter on Scriptures. The following notes were taken from an actual study. They are thorough and complete. The study was completed in three hours and the lady was baptized two weeks later, as she desired to study further privately. In such a case, it is wise to encourage the prospect to be in attendance at the worship services during the intervening time and also wise to call in about a week and ask about the progress of study and ask if any help is needed. After you have read the chapter on Scriptures, it would be wise to return to these sample

notes and compare. After you have made your first study,
it would also be wise to compare your notes to these to
see how thorough you were. It is hard to write and talk
and concentrate, but that is what must be done. Did anyone ever give you directions to a certain address? Have
you ever forgotten to write the directions down only to
discover later that you wished you had? Here we are instructing a person in the direction to heaven, as given by
God. Writing the Scriptures down will be a great asset.

**Help the prospect receive the same honor as that be-
stowed upon the Bereans.** Acts 17:11: "These (Bereans)
were more noble than those in Thessalonica, in that they
received the word with all readiness of mind, and searched
the Scriptures daily, whether those things were so." When
we leave notes and encourage them to study and search
we are encouraging them to do as the Bereans did and to
be just as "noble."

GOAL: Eternal Life

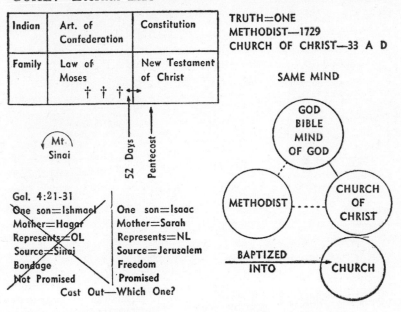

Indian	Art. of Confederation	Constitution
Family	Law of Moses † † †	New Testament of Christ

TRUTH=ONE
METHODIST—1729
CHURCH OF CHRIST—33 A D

SAME MIND

Mt. Sinai

52 Days   Pentecost

Gal. 4:21-31
One son=Ishmael
Mother=Hagar
Represents=OL
Source=Sinai
Bondage
Not Promised

One son=Isaac
Mother=Sarah
Represents=NL
Source=Jerusalem
Freedom
Promised

Cast Out—Which One?

GOD BIBLE MIND OF GOD

METHODIST

CHURCH OF CHRIST

BAPTIZED INTO

CHURCH

Col. 2:14	Acts 3:19	Col. 1:18	Eph. 5:19
Heb. 8:6-7	———	Eph. 4:4	Col. 3:16
Rom. 15:4	Matt. 10:32-33	Matt. 16:18	Rev. 22:18-19
2 Tim. 3:16-17	Rom. 10:9-10	Acts 2:47	1 Cor. 4:6
2 Pet. 1:3	Matt. 16:15-17	Acts 20:28	Gal. 1:6-9
John 10:1	Acts 8:37	Rom. 16:16	———
John 10:10		Acts 11:26	Rom. 12:1
John 14:6	Matt. 28:18-19		Titus 2:11-14
Matt. 7:21-23	Mark 16:15-16	Eph. 1:3	Rev. 2:10
Matt. 7:13-14 Few	Acts 2:37-47	———	
Matt. 28:18-20 All	Acts 8:35-39	Matt. 26:26-29	Jas. 4:17
	Eph. 4:5	Luke 22:19-20	
John 14:15	Rom. 6:3-4	John 6:53-54	John 14:15
John 3:16	Gal. 3:27	Acts 20:7	
John 8:24	1 Cor. 12:13		Law to the
Heb. 11:6		1 Cor. 16:1-2	Fallen Christian
	Col. 3:17		for husband
Luke 13:3	John 17:11	Acts 2:42	James 5:16
Acts 17:30	1 Cor. 1:10-13	1 Tim. 2:15	Acts 8:22
2 Cor. 7:10	1 Cor. 3:3-6	Phil. 1:9	Rev. 2:5
		1 Thess. 5:17	

DO ALL ↑ HIS WILL:

1. Believe
2. Repent

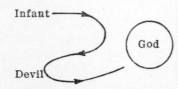

Infant →
God
Devil →

3. Confess: Before Men with mouth
4. Be Baptized=Remission of sins
5. Do ALL in his name
6. Partake of Lord's Supper each first day of each week
7. Give as prospered
8. Forsake not assembly (Assemble with saints)
9. Study (continue in apostles' doctrine)
10. Pray
11. Praise
12. Be Servant—Serve—Sacrifice
13. Deny worldliness
14. Deny worldly lusts
15. Live soberly
16. Live righteously
17. Be zealous
18. Love—keep commands

GIVE

OL	NL
$50.00 10%=$5.00	$50.00 As Prospered

GROW—$1.00 then $2.00 then $5.00 until sacrifice

PUT GOD FIRST

BUDGET

1. God
2. Food
3. Insurance
4. Clothing
5. Drugs

	Voice	Mechanical Instrument
Speak	CAN	CANNOT
Teach	CAN	CANNOT
Admonish	CAN	CANNOT

Disciples=Christian

No Christian Church **Then**

No Disciples Church **Then**

No Brethren Church **Then**

No Lutheran Church **Then**

No Anybody's Church

Individuals=Christian
Collection of Obedient
Individuals Equals
Body or Church
of Christ

Progress Report

Successful businesses keep going forward by requiring progress reports from personnel. It is a known fact in business that workers who analyze themselves periodically, and who strive to correct the weak points as shown by the cold facts on paper, make more rapid progress than workers who refuse to look into their own lives with a view toward helping themselves. The following chart is presented with the aim in mind of helping you to analyze yourself and to progress so you will be able to study with different types of people in different situations, adjusting yourself to talk to different personalities, and still just present the Bible in its simplicity. This chart should help you to realize if anything is lacking in your approach, your study and your closing—being at ease in a study will come as you familiarize yourself with various Scriptures. You may want to add a few thoughts to the chart for you personally, but try to fill it out—not with every study, but it is wise to do so for at least the first six study periods and at varying intervals thereafter.

Progress Report

1. Personal Worker's name _____

2. Prospect's name _____

   Address _____ Phone _____

   Age (approximate) ____ Church affiliation _____
   (These are helpful, not a must)

   Date of study _____ Hour of study _____

   First contact _____

3. Setting: (Environment, items taken) _____

   _____

4. State as near as possible the words used in gaining the appointment: _____

   _____

5. State as near as possible the words used in transition from the introduction to the actual study: _____
_____

6. Your first impression of the prospect: _____

7. General trend of study: _____

8. Results: _____

9. State as near as possible the words used in calling for obedience (if called for): _____
_____

10. State your honest opinion of how you did; listing good and bad points: _____
_____
_____

11. List the things you should do differently next time:
_____

CLOSING

Need For Closing

There is a great need that we learn how to close our study so as to gain obedience. If we do not close the study, then our job is just one-half finished. A doctor that can make an incision and cannot suture the opening is not very much of a doctor. To lead a person near unto salvation and fall just short of it is not good. Many persons lost their lives after walking miles and miles and day after day during the western march and then falling, too exhausted to carry on. Years later their skeletons were found within a short distance of water and food. Many people can talk to another person about Christ but never cause him to obey the gospel. While I was holding a meeting in Arkansas, I listened to a man tell about a fishing trip. They laid out their fishing lines, and just before midnight checked them. There were three hooks and only one large fish. They decided that since they had caught one they had him hooked and would not remove him—but leave the line in the water to attract fish to the two remaining hooks. When they took in the line in the morning the two hooks were still empty and the fish that was on the other hook had worked loose. So many of us do not make the closing when the closing could be made. There is a great need for us to learn how to close every study in the most profitable way.

Closing Attitude

The manner of coming to a close and calling for obedience is so important that if it is not done right we can undo all that has been accomplished beforehand. Near the end of the Scriptures, we should cause our voices to become lower and more persuasive. An abrupt change would only tend to do harm because it would be noticeable that

you were going to "push." We should never push. Paul
said, "I persuade men." To accomplish this, we must appeal to their wants, appeal to happiness, appeal to emotion,
appeal to intellect, appeal to their strong motives. (Children, age, future). Appeal to imagination and create a
vivid picture. The power of persuasion is best demonstrated through questions. When you are asked when to
obey, you might ask, "If you needed an operation, how
long would you wait?" The following illustration is given
to show the value of persuasion: During World War I,
many of the great industrialists were gathered together
while Lord George appealed to them to pool their secrets
to provide the maximum amount of guns and ammunition.
Many of the industrialists refused to do so, thinking in
terms of their future after the war. Lord George used
the power of persuasion by asking them in a low, appealing voice, "Have you forgotten that your sons in this very
moment are being killed in hundreds of thousands? Your
sons, your brothers, boys at the dawn of manhood are being wiped out by the thousands. Gentlemen, give me guns,
help those boys and our women and children. Give me
your guns to help them." This illustration was taken from
the book, "Mirrors of Downing Street," pages 5 and 6, G.
P. Putnam's Sons. Sincere desire for the salvation of the
souls of men will help us have the proper earnestness and
persuasiveness. Usually it is wise to call attention to the
all important question prior to James 4:17 in the designated series. (Of course other Scriptures may follow for
persuasion purposes). The conversation may go like this.
"There is an important question that I want to ask you
but first may we turn and read James 4:17 for it has a
bearing on the answer that you will want to give?" After
the prospect reads that Scripture, you may say, "Does it
help to know what to do and not to do it?" Allow him to
give an answer and then ask "Wouldn't you like to do
what you have studied here?" If he answers yes, ask

him, "When would you like to do this—tonight or Sunday?" If he says, "I don't know," then review and reason what he has to gain by obedience, what he has to lose by refusing to obey and then cause him to read John 14:15, after which you ask, "If you love the Lord, what should you do?" If he answers no to the question, "Wouldn't you like to do what you have studied here?" ask him, "What is it that prevents you from doing this?" This will give you the hindering cause and you can work to overcome it with some of the things listed later in this chapter, "Closing Appeals Over Objections."

Persuasion

Persuasion is Scriptural. Often persuasion is objected to by those who may not know how to justify the absence of it or by those who think that the individual is being pushed or would be baptized prematurely. Of course when you are studying with an individual you can gauge the persuasion angle—if he is lacking in knowledge, take more time and teach him further, however, so much of the time the delay in obedience is not because of knowledge but some other detail we can help him to overcome. In our homes, we persuade our children to do certain tasks and call this "training", knowing full well they do not know how to do everything. Sometimes we persuade them with a switch. Of course, this can never be the case in causing people to obey the gospel, but the proper kind of persuasion is necessary. Paul said in 2 Corinthians 5:11, "Knowing therefore the terror of the Lord, we persuade men." If Paul was not persuading men, then what did he mean? How did Paul persuade men? In Acts 13:40-41, Paul told those at Antioch of Pisidia, "Beware therefore, lest that come upon you which is spoken of in the prophets: Behold, ye despisers, and wonder, and perish; For I work a work in your days, a work which ye shall in no wise believe, though a man declare it unto you." Paul warned

them here of the destruction ahead if they refused his
preaching and also pointed out the foolishness of hearing
the word declared and in no wise believing it. The application of this persuasion is needed today and is Scriptural
by example. In 2 Corinthians 6:1-2 we read another example of Paul's persuasion, "We then as workers together
with him beseech you also that ye receive not the grace
of God in vain (for he saith, I have heard thee in a time
accepted, and in the day of salvation have I succored thee:
now is the acceptable time; behold, now is the day of salvation"). Here we learn that Paul "entreated" them to
make that day the day of their salvation. Peter persuaded men in Acts 2 by causing them to be pricked in their
hearts and asking a question to know what to do to remove their guilt. He called for their obedience by saying,
"Repent and **be baptized everyone of you** in the name of
Jesus Christ for the remission of sins." He did not stop
with this persuasion but continued (some think this continuing is unscriptural, but notice) in Acts 2:40: "And
with many other words did he testify, and exhort, saying,
save yourselves from this untoward generation." The result of this persuasion was gratifying. It will be today if
we will follow this Scriptural example. Persuasion is sometimes limited to asking for obedience one time by many,
but here in Acts 2 Peter did not stop his persuasion until
they obeyed the Gospel—certainly not all, but more than
had he not continued his call and reasoning for obedience.
This persuasion should continue until you see you cannot
do good. It should not continue to a point where we are
unwelcome or have done harm. Recognizing that can happen, the personal worker must learn how to accomplish the
closing scenes of the study in the most effective way.

Sometimes it is necessary to persuade the personal worker to be persuasive. It is recognized that this act of influ-
encing the mind by reasoning at the close of a sermon is a
must. So is it at the close of a study. I heard of a preach-

er who was not persuading men, and the elders asked him to do so. At the close of the next sermon he stood at the front and said, "I persuade you to accept the invitation of Christ." Persuading is not an act of using the word, but is doing that which is persuasion. Persuasion in many instances is persistence. Many salespersons have called upon their clients for years before making a sale, yet the sale when made amounted to a large enough amount to warrant the constant effort. The timing of the closing is important. Certainly in an actual study, we should not wait years. Usually it is wise to wind up the actual study with the closing Scriptures and questions suggested, but should it take longer, don't give up easily. If the worker will consider himself in the prospect's place and understand as he is thinking, it will assist in making the final appeal for action. An account was related to me of an insurance man who had a very dear friend. He would visit the friend time after time, explaining various insurance policies to him and keeping him up to date with the latest clauses in all of the policies. Much time and effort was spent in this friend's home. Then one day he heard that his friend had purchased a large insurance policy from another insurance man, a man who until that day had been a rank stranger to him. The first insurance man approached his friend and asked him why he had not purchased such a policy from him and the friend replied, "You never asked me to buy one from you." We may visit and teach the Bible, but usually there is no action until we ask definite questions concerning obedience.

Some Closing Appeals Over Objections

It is important that we find the barrier or obstacle standing in the way of obedience. We make a great error by failing to appeal for action even after we hear "no" or see a refusal to answer. We need to find the cause of refusal and try to remove it. A doctor tries to find the cause of pains and if it be necessary remove that cause by an operation or medicine. To find out why, we must ask for that reason. There is no way of reading minds, therefore, simply ask, "May I ask what keeps you from obeying these truths you have studied and acknowledged as right?" Some of these answers will be false barriers and others honest. Treat them alike in most instances, showing the fallacy of each excuse:

EXCUSE	SUGGESTED REPLY
1. "I fear I do not know enough." or "I will when I learn more."	1. Underlying this excuse is the honest desire often to wait until he can guard himself from the questionings of others about his actions.
	2. Compliment him for his desire to know more of the gospel and state that you can see how he feels.
	3. Review the lesson step by step as: "What did Jesus tell us to do to enter Heaven?" Receive the correct answer and then ask, "What is His will about belief?" "Repentance?"; "Confession?"; "Baptism?"; "Proper name to wear?"; "Which right church?"; "What about the Lord's Supper?"; "Study?"; "Prayer?"; "Praise?" Since he understands these he should do these and learn more after baptism. Show him from Matthew 28:18-20 that teaching comes after baptism as well as before. Tell him you as a personal worker still would not be a Christian had you waited until you knew everything—for you are learning new things each day.
2. "I am afraid of what the people will say."	1. Underlying this excuse is the fear of persecution.
	2. Matthew 5:11-12, "Blessed are ye, when men shall revile you, and

persecute you, and shall say all manner of evil against you falsely, for my sake. Rejoice, and be exceeding glad, for great is your reward in heaven: for so persecuted they the prophets which were before you."

3. 2 Timothy 3:12, "Yea, and all that will live godly in Christ Jesus shall suffer persecution."

4. 1 Peter 4:16, "Yet if any man suffer as a Christian, let him not be ashamed; but let him glorify God on this behalf."

5. Revelation 2:10, ". . . Be thou faithful unto death, and I will give thee a crown of life."

3. "I do not know what I really want, I am so confused."

1. Review the third suggestion of number one above and then ask, "Do you want to please the Lord the way you admit is right and go to heaven?" Ask after the review of each subject, "Are you confused on faith (others)?" If he is, you should be able to find out and thus overcome the problem.

2. Ask, "Is there anything greater than your eternal soul's salvation?" after reading Matthew 16: 26, "For what is a man profited, if he shall gain the whole world, and lose his own soul? or what shall a man give in exchange for his soul?"

4. "I am afraid I cannot remain a Christian"

or

"The Christian life is too hard."

1. Either the individual thinks he has tried and failed or feels that he will not try hard enough.

2. Always ask, "Have you ever given the Lord a real chance to help you remain a Christian?" Point out experience is the best test and remember the slogan: "Taste and Tell." This excuse makes

very little impression upon the true Christian. "If you were a Christian, I'm sure such an excuse would phase you little. Those outside of Christ understand little until they have tasted."

3. Romans 4:21, "And being fully persuaded, that what he had promised, he was able also to perform."

4. 1 Corinthians 10:13, "There hath no temptation taken you but such as is common to man: but God is faithful, who will not suffer you to be tempted above that ye are able; but will with the temptation also make a way to escape, that ye may be able to bear it."

5. Philippians 1:6, "Being confident of this very thing, that he which hath begun a good work in you will perform it until the day of Jesus Christ."

6. Philippians 4:13, "I can do all things through Christ which strengtheneth me."

7. 1 Timothy 1:12, "And I thank Christ Jesus our Lord, who hath enabled me, for that he counted me faithful . . . "

8. Hebrews 7:25, "Wherefore he is able also to save them to the uttermost that come unto God by him . . ."

5. "My mother's religion is good enough for me."

or

"What will happen to my good and honest parents who did not know of this way to heaven?"

1. Of course, you should have shown them that difference through your study but sometimes they cling to this for an excuse.

2. Ask, "Did you find the Bible approving your mother's religion?"

3. Point out that you cannot change the destiny of any who have gone before.

4. Always tell him that the souls of

parents (or others mentioned) are in the hands of a merciful God and we cannot change it. WE must do what we know to do.

5. Ask, "If your parents knew what you know, don't you think they would have done what God wants them to do or encouraged you to do the same thing?"

6. Ask, "If you are wrong, would you want your children to follow you?"

6. "I want to ask my preacher."

or

"That is the way YOU interpret it."

1. This is the same as saying, "My preacher is as smart as you (and honest) and he sees it this way or that." Reply, "I know of others differing from both of us. What shall we use as the final judge concerning all of us?"

2. 2 Peter 1:20, "Knowing this first, that no prophecy of the Scripture is of any private interpretation."

3. Suggest that he himself has had many years in which to drink in the teachings of his preacher (preaching), then ask, "Did he ever preach such as we have studied right from the Bible? If not, why not?"

4. Point out that no preacher, including church of Christ preachers, nor yourself is as smart as God. Isaiah 55:8-9, "For my thoughts are not your thoughts, neither your ways my ways, saith Jehovah. For as the heavens are higher than the earth, so are my ways higher than your ways, and my thoughts than your thoughts."

5. Ask, "Is the preacher God or is the author of what we have studied God?"

6. If these fail, as a last resort, insist he see his preacher and compare what he says with the Bible.

7. "I am presently satisfied with my religion."
   (or baptism, etc.)
      or
   "I feel I am already saved."

1. If this comes at the close, little can be accomplished. We have failed in our presentation or they are blind to the facts.

2. 2 Corinthians 10:12, 18, "For we dare not make ourselves of the number, or compare ourselves with some that commend themselves: but they, measuring themselves by themselves, and comparing themselves among themselves, are not wise . . . For not he that commendeth himself is approved, but whom the Lord commendeth."

3. Find something they are not satisfied with, such as job, car, clothes, etc., and ask, "Are you satisfied with your car (etc.)?" "Are you not always trying to improve yourself?"

4. Ask, "How can we be satisfied when we know we are not safe or have left undone the commands of the Lord?" Review James 4: 17 in this connection.

5. State, "Man should not try to please himself, Jesus did not." John 5:30 "I seek not mine own will, but the will of the Father which hath sent me."

6. Luke 16:15 "Ye are they which justify yourselves before men; but God knoweth your hearts: for that which is highly esteemed among men is abomination in the sight of God."

8. "I do not want to make a change."
      or
   "I think I've already made the right choice."

1. "Please show me the Scripture backing up your choice."

2. "Why change religion? To be right. If we travel the same route to and from work every day— never looking for a change—we

would be confused if a new short cut road were made—we would travel the same old way to be consistent. Our aim is not to proselyte you from one church to another but to cause you to obey the truth which is right and which will make you free."

3. "Is that choice as you've studied here right from the Bible?"

9. "You are right but I still think all of the churches are right too."

1. "Please continue your study and show me the Scripture that approves of wearing different names, allows division, allows men to speak different doctrines, allows many various ways of worshipping."

2. "If we are right and you fail to do those things right, you would be wrong wouldn't you in light of Luke 6:46?" "Why call ye me, Lord, Lord, and do not the things which I say?"

10. "I do not see how a change will make me live any longer."

1. Underlying this is that basic appeal to live longer.

2. Matthew 25:46 "And these shall go away into everlasting punishment: but the righteous into life eternal."

3. Ask, "If heaven is without end, don't you want to live longer in it in bliss rather than just as long but in punishment?"

11. "There are some things I still would like to do."
   or
"I have to give up too many things."
   or
"I have to surrender too much."

1. This is similar to a statement I heard one time: "My husband depends upon me in his business. I must go to social affairs where they drink. I cannot give that up for it would hurt his business."

2. Point out that Felix was afraid to give up many things and thus never found a convenient season in which to become a Christian. Agrippa was "almost a Christian" and almost is but to fail.

3. Luke 12:21 "So is he that layeth up treasure for himself, and is not rich toward God."

4. Luke 14:33 "So likewise, whosoever he be of you that forsaketh not all that he hath, he cannot be my disciple."

5. Galations 6:7 "Be not deceived; God is not mocked: for whatsoever a man soweth, that shall he also reap."

6. 1 Timothy 5:6 "But she that liveth in pleasure is dead while she liveth."

7. 2 Thessalonians 2:12 "That they all might be damned who believe not the truth, but had pleasure in unrighteousness."

8. 1 Peter 2:11 "I beseech you as strangers and pilgrims, abstain from fleshly lusts, which war against the soul."

12. "I think hell is right here on earth."

1. Previous study and faith should have removed this objection. There are some who will hold out excuse just to have an argument for not accepting the truth.

2. Matthew 7:13-14 "Hell is easily found." "Enter ye in at the strait gate: for wide is the gate, and broad is the way, that leadeth to destruction, and many there be which go in thereat: Because strait is the gate, and narrow is the way, which leadeth unto life, and few there be that find it."

3. Luke 12:5 "I will forewarn you whom ye shall fear: fear him, which after he hath killed hath power to cast into hell: yea, I say unto you, fear him."

4. 2 Thessalonians 1:7-9 "And to you who are troubled rest with us, when the Lord Jesus shall be

revealed from heaven with his mighty angels, in flaming fire taking vengeance on them that know not God and obey not the gospel of our Lord Jesus Christ: who shall be punished with everlasting destruction . . ."

5. Revelation 20:15 "And whosoever was not found written in the book of life was cast into the lake of fire."

6. Revelation 21:8 "But the fearful, and unbelieving, and the abominable, and murderers, and whoremongers, and sorcerers, and idolators, and all liars, shall have their part in the lake which burning with fire and brimstone: which is the second death." "As we know of the first death and God revealed that — don't you think God can reveal and bring to pass the second death?"

7. Hell cannot be on the earth for this reason: 2 Peter 3:10, 12 "But the day of the Lord will come as a thief in the night: in the which the heavens shall pass away with a great noise, and the elements shall melt with fervent heat, and earth also and the works that are therein shall be burned up . . . looking for and hasting unto the coming of the day of God, wherein the heavens being on fire shall be dissolved, and the elements shall melt with fervent heat."

13. "All of your religion is 'Don't do this or that.'"

1. "Do you know of anything in life that does not have certain prohibitions?"

2. If we do not correct this statement, we allow him to keep a wrong impression. James 1:25 "But whoso looketh into the per-

fect law of liberty, and continueth therein, he being not a forgetful hearer, but a doer of the work, this man shall be blessed in his deed."

3. "For every positive statement there is a negative prohibition. All of life is under a law of inclusion and exclusion. When we say that we LOVE God—hate of God is prohibited."

4. "All religious prohibitions are of God—not man." 2 John 9 "Whosoever transgresseth, and abideth not in the doctrine of Christ, hath not God. He that abideth in the doctrine of Christ, he hath both the Father and the Son." "Note here the positive and negative of God's will."

5. This objection implies constant condemnation. How may we eliminate this condemnation? Romans 8:1 "There is therefore now NO CONDEMNATION to them which are in Christ Jesus, who walk not after the flesh, but after the Spirit."

14. "Your religion is just a blind acceptance."

or

"There are too many mysteries about your religion and following the Bible."

1. Point out that many things of life are accepted blindly and that we do not refuse to use them. "Do we know how to explain electricity—yet we go ahead and use it. Do we act by faith when we eat food? How certain are we that it does not contain poison?"

2. "Yes, life has many unknowables, but John 20:30-31 says 'And many other signs truly did Jesus in the presence of his disciples, which are not written in this book: but these are written, that ye might believe that Jesus is the Christ, the Son of God; and that

believing ye might have life through his name'."

3. Deuteronomy 29:29 "The secret things belong unto the Lord our God; but those things which are revealed belong unto us and to our children forever . . . "

4. 2 Corinthians 5:7 "For we walk by faith, and not by sight."

5. 1 Corinthians 13:2, 12 "Though I have the gift of prophecy, and understand all mysteries, and all knowledge; and though I have all faith, so that I could remove mountains, and HAVE NOT CHARITY, I am nothing." "For now we see through a glass darkly: but then face to face: now I know in part, but then shall I know even as also I am known."

6. John 13:7 "Jesus answered and said unto him, What I do thou knowest not now; but thou shalt know hereafter."

7. "Religion is not a 'better felt than told' religion. It must be based upon intellectual acceptance and what we do must have a 'thus saith the Lord'." 1 Peter 3:15 ". . . be ready always to give an answer to every man that asketh you a reason of the hope that is in you . . . "

15. The indifferent.

1. "Are you aware of death?" They cannot be indifferent toward that fact.

2. Ask, "Must we prepare for other eventualities one way or the other?" Matthew 1:24-26 "If any man will come after me, let him deny himself, and take up his cross, and follow me. For whosoever will save his life shall lose it; and whosoever will lose his life for my sake shall find it. For

what is a man profited, if he shall gain the whole world, and lose his own soul? or what shall a man give in exchange for his soul?"

3. Try to find the reason for the indifference and follow with one of the other suggested closing appeals.

16. "I just don't see it YOUR way."

1. Of course, proper presentation of the Bible lesson should have prevented such an excuse.

2. "YOUR way indicates that we should point out that we as man do not have a way." A review of some of the earlier points to show CHRIST'S WAY would help.

3. If this is the final conclusion, little can be done. Suggest he continue his study and offer to help him but have him call you for the appointment. Your constant prodding after this will do little good.

17. "I just do not want to do those things but I do love Jesus."

1. Ask, "What do those who love Jesus do?" Read John 14:15 in this connection "If ye love me, keep my commandments." "The question is, Do you love him enough to do his commandments?"

18. "I want to improve first and if I can then I'll do these things."

1. "Jesus will improve us completely if we will let Him. We only improve ourselves partially—Jesus came to such persons as yourself." Matthew 9:3 " . . . I came not to call the righteous, but sinners. . . . "

2. "Have you succeeded up till now by yourself?" Matthew 6:33 "But seek ye first his kingdom, and his righteousness; and all these things shall be added unto you." "Your complete improvement

comes after you put something else first."

19. "God is love, He will not punish anyone."

1. "God condemns only those who condemn themselves by not following His will."

2. Mark 16:16 "He that believeth and is baptized shall be saved; but he that believeth not shall be condemned."

3. Luke 13:3 "I tell you, Nay; but, except ye repent, ye shall all in like manner perish." "Who is going to cause this perishing?"

4. 2 Thessalonians 1:8-9 ". . . taking vengeance on them that know not God and that obey not the gospel of our Lord Jesus Christ, who shall be punished with everlasting destruction from the presence of the Lord, and from the glory of his power."

20. "What if there is someone that I cannot forgive nor feel right toward?"

1. Ask, "You must forgive if you expect Jesus to forgive you—do you expect him to forgive your sins?"

2. Matthew 6:15 "But if ye forgive not men their trespasses, neither will your Father forgive your trespasses."

3. Philippians 4:13 "I can do all things (even forgive - IRS) through Christ which strengtheneth me."

4. Ephesians 4:32 "And be ye kind one to another, tenderhearted, forgiving one another, even as God for Christ's sake hath forgiven you."

21. "I have plenty of time."
or
"I'm not ready."
or
"I'll wait until a more convenient season."

1. State, "This is contrary to your own witness for you know people are dying every day and some day will be our day of death."

2. Hebrews 9:27 ". . . it is appointed unto men once to die, but after this the judgment."

3. Romans 13:11 "And that know-

ing the time, that now it is high
time to awake out of sleep: for
now is our salvation nearer than
when we believed."

4. 2 Corinthians 6:2 ". . . behold,
now is the accepted time; behold,
now is the day of salvation."

5. Matthew 24:44 "Therefore be ye
also ready: for in such an hour
as ye think not the Son of man
cometh."

22. "It is too late **and**
besides   I'm   too
mean."

1. John 9:4 "I must work the works
of him that sent me, while it is
day; the night cometh, when no
man can work."

2. 1 John 1:9 "If we confess our
sins, he is faithful and just to
forgive us our sins, and to cleanse
us from ALL unrighteousness."

3. "Is your sin comparable to kill-
ing Jesus?" Point out that those
who killed Jesus were forgiven.
Acts 2.

4. "Are we different from Paul in
Acts 22:16?" "And now why tar-
riest thou? arise, and be baptized, and wash away thy sins,
calling on the name of the Lord."

5. Romans 10:13 "For whosoever
shall call upon the name of the
Lord shall be saved." Be sure
not to leave the impression that
this "calling" is just verbal appeal. Show them how to "call"
upon the name of the Lord.

23. "I do not feel that
way."
        or
"How   am   I   sup-
posed to feel?"

1. "Feeling is a result and not a
cause. Feeling is fickle. Concerning the same item, two persons
may drink whiskey (cause) and
feel (result) differently. One is
jolly and the other wants to kill.
Concerning the same item but the
same person, feeling is also fickle. Today you have $100.00 in

the bank and feel that you want to save it — tomorrow you see something that you would like to have and feel that you should take the money out of the bank and spend it."

2. Hebrews 10:36 "For ye have need of patience, that after ye have done the will of God, ye might receive the promise."

3. Acts 5:32 "And we are his witness of these things; and so is also the Holy Ghost, whom God hath given to them that obey him."

4. 1 John 5:2 "By this we know that we love the children of God, when we love God and keep his commandments."

5. Luke 6:46 "And why call ye me, Lord, Lord and do not the things which I say?" State, "All of these have to do with doing his will and nothing about the way we feel—is that correct?"

24. "There are too many hypocrites in the church already."
     or
     "I am as good as many."

1. "If your intentions are to become another hypocrite, you should not go through the forms of obedience."

2. Matthew 7:1, 5 "Judge not, that ye be not judged . . . Thou hypocrite, first cast out the beam out of thine own eye; and then shalt thou see clearly to cast out the mote out of thy brother's eye."

3. Luke 16:15 "Ye are they which justify yourselves before men; but God knowest your hearts; for that which is highly esteemed among men is abomination in the sight of God."

4. Romans 2:5, 6 "But after thy hardness and impenitent heart, treasurest up unto thyself wrath against the day of wrath and rev-

elation of the righteous judgment of God; who will render to every man according to his deeds."

5. Romans 14:12 "So then every one of us shall give account of himself to God."

6. 2 Corinthians 5:10 "For we must all appear before the judgment seat of Christ; that every one may receive the things done in his body, according to that he hath done, whether it be good or bad."

25. If they cling to a previous religious action not wanting to admit they are wrong such as: "I was baptized because I was already saved," etc.

1. Review whatever action they cling to in light of the Scriptures.

2. "Is there an example of anyone in the Bible ever being baptized because he was already saved?" Review the Scriptures on baptism and ask, "Do you still feel the way you do in light of these lessons from heaven?"

26. Final appeal.

1. Review the lesson step by step as: "What did Jesus tell us to do to enter heaven?" Receive the right answer and then ask "What is His will about belief?"—"Repentance?" — "Confession?" — "Baptism?" — "Proper name to wear?" — "Which is the right church?" — "What about the Lord's Supper?" — "Study?" — "Prayer?" — "Praise?" If these t h i n g s are understood ask, "Should you do these and learn more after baptism? You can only do that which you know to do."

2. "Would you like to die in your present condition?"

3. Leave notes—suggest they study them. If they have any questions, make them feel free to ask you about them later.

4. Offer to study with them another time.
5. Make another appointment before leaving if mutual.
6. Not all are successful — Jesus Christ taught in the individual situation to the rich young ruler and the ruler "went away sorrowful," Do not force a decision but do "PERSUADE." You do your work and Jesus Christ will do his. 1 Corinthians 3:6 "increase" and Acts 2:47 "added."

"Off Hours" Baptismal Service

There are some advantages in offering to help the prospect to be baptized immediately. First, it is Scriptural by teaching and by example. It removes the fear that sometimes might be connected with a larger audience. The teaching is fresh on the mind immediately after such a study. To suggest that it removes numbers of people does not mean that there can be no one there. If he requests, then certainly baptize him with just the studying group there, otherwise, it is wise to call your wife, an elder, or some close friends of the one being baptized. Usually they call others. When the prospect does not ask that it be limited, usually twenty to thirty are always in attendance.

What should be done at such a baptismal service? What should be done at any baptismal service? Actually the baptism is the important and necessary thing at that time, however, it will create a closeness and warmth of feeling to have a few songs and prayers. One man that had been baptized privately attended the baptism of another man later. That night he remarked, "I believe these week-day services are more meaningful than the regular ones." Usually it is wise to set a time. This allows those called to come if they can. If you have finished the study at 8:30 p.m. and the prospect has indicated his desire to be baptized, you could suggest 9:00 p.m. At the building, have all, including the one to be baptized, sit in a group. You can be very informal, yet have a serious service. Choose two or three songs, make a few remarks or read some Scriptures, then have a prayer. While the prospect is preparing, the others may sing or sit quietly meditating. After the baptism, someone in the group in front usually words another prayer. Usually without any instruction, those gathered will greet with much kindness and affection the obedient soul who has put on his Lord in baptism. It is truly a time of rejoicing—never let it become so commonplace in your life that you cannot congratulate the one baptized.

We do not have to wait until the whole congregation is assembled to baptize people. By tradition, we have grown to depend upon three times: Sunday morning and evening, and then the mid-week service. Other times than this are unscriptural in the eyes of some. On one occasion, I had been studying with a man and his wife, and had told them that I would be happy to baptize them at any time. They had been shown where the Philippian Jailor was baptized about midnight and where the Ethiopian eunuch was baptized in a desert area on the way to Gaza from Jerusalem— evidently without an assemblage to witness. They called one evening and asked to be baptized that night, which was the evening prior to the beginning of a meeting scheduled for that congregation. I was happy to hear their desire and baptized them that evening. Several of the brethren asked me why we did not wait until the next morning, suggesting that this would have been a wonderful way to have begun the meeting. That in itself would have been a wrong motive. There is no Scriptural authority to wait until a certain time, but that is an aspect the denominations have added. They make a habit of waiting until a certain Sunday and have a religious rite for all collected over a period of time. What if they should die before the appointed day? Let us be consistent in doing what they did in the New Testament and let us practice it just that way.

PREPARING THE INDIVIDUAL TO ACCEPT THE BIBLE AS THE WORD OF GOD

Need of this Preparation

Man cannot have the Bible guiding him unless he believes that it is the authority of God. If you are talking with a person who does not believe the Bible to be the Word of God, then he must be helped to upset his previous beliefs in rejecting the Bible or he will never accept the Bible as his authority. "A man convinced against his will remains of the same opinion still" is very true. If one book is as good as another, as one church may be considered as good as another in the eyes of your prospect, you cannot cause him to listen to what God has to say in the Bible alone, no more than you can take one of his books and use it as a guide if you do not accept it as such. We then of necessity must show that the Bible is the Word of God and the only Word of God. Of all of the books available, to which shall we listen? In the realm of religion there are many other books that guide the religious thoughts of men. Such books as Rig-Veda, the Zend-Avesta (the book of Zoroastrianism), the Buddhist writings, Tao-teh-king writings of Taoism, Book of Mormon, Science and Health with Key to the Scriptures, Confucian Texts, and the Koran (book of authority in Mohammedanism) are used as a guide by some people. Many do not accept the Bible as the Word of God and excuse themselves on the basis that these other books do exist. No doubt you can see the problem that exists. FROM HOUSE TO HOUSE is intended primarily to help you in studying with people who do accept the Bible as the word of God and are religiously wrong; however, as stated above, some individuals do not accept the Bible as the revealed word of God. The objections to the Bible are in so many varied areas that it would be necessary to study the particular line that is taken by the objector. This chapter is designed to introduce you to various problems and to suggest a possible method or approach, but if you are interested in preparing yourself specifically for this type of study, it would be in order to read several books on Apologetics or Christian evidences to help you to be more aware of particular problems.

Other books cannot prove to be the Word of God. An examination of any book other than the Bible will show the absence of a Supreme Mind—only the Bible has been proven through the ages to be without contradiction. A comparison of any other book with the Bible will quickly show which book was guided by a Supreme Being. These other works take liberties not granted by God, show contradiction within themselves and with the Bible itself, contradict facts of history and life and above all have not proved outstanding. The Asiatic books purporting to be from inspired minds are readily known to be contradictory. Their hopes are not based upon prophecy and its fulfillment, nor proof that a perfect founder has prepared the way toward an eternal dwelling, nor that their supposed Saviour has been victorious over death. There are two books which contend to be compatible with the Scriptures. However, an examination of both of these will show the fallibility in human minds, thus we can conclude that the mind of man cannot compare with the mind of God. We shall examine these two books briefly in the following section.

Examination of the Book of Mormon:

1. **The books of the Mormons try to remove the authority from the Bible:** The Doctrine and Covenants is considered to be another revelation and an authority with the Mormon people, and Section 84:57 reads "And they shall remain under this condemnation until they repent and remember the new covenant, even the Book of Mormon, and the former commandments which I have given them."

This accredits a new covenant other than that given in the Bible—and would make the New Covenant of the Bible NOT THE New Covenant. Read Hebrews 8:6-7, 13.

2. **The Bible makes no room for other revelations.** The Old Testament approved of the New Testament yet to come, while the New Testament approved of the Old Testament, and neither looks forward to any other publication, stating within that they are complete. It is true that all that Jesus did is not written in the Bible (John 20:30), but the following verse tells us that enough is written for us to heed and thereby gain eternal life: "But these are written, that ye might believe that Jesus is the Christ, the Son of God, and that believing ye might have life through His name." (John 20:31) We are warned against having other revelations or gospels in Galatians 1:6-9: "I marvel that ye are so soon removed from him that called you into the grace of Christ unto another gospel; which is not another; but there be some that trouble you, and would pervert the gospel of Christ. But though we, or an angel from heaven, preach any other gospel unto you than that which we have preached unto you, let him be accursed." So complete is the Bible that it is able to furnish man completely unto every good work. 2 Timothy 3:16-17. The gospel alone is the power unto salvation—Romans 1:16. "All truth" as relates to the salvation of men and women was given to the apostles of the first centutry. Read John 14:15-26; 16:13; Ephesians 3:1-15; Jude 23. In 2 Peter 1:3 we read, "All things that pertain unto life and godliness" have been given. The Old Testament (Deuteronomy 4:2) teaches us we are not to add to the Scriptures nor to take away from them, and the same thought is borne out in the New Testament (1 Corinthians 4:6 and Revelation 22:18-19).

3. **The book of Mormon is contradictory to the Bible.** Micah 5:2 tells us where Jesus is to be born: "But thou, **Bethlehem**, Ephratah, though thou be little among the

thousands of Judah, yet out of thee shall he come forth unto me that is to be ruler in Israel, whose goings forth have been from of old, from everlasting." Notice where the book of Mormon says Jesus will be born: Alma 7:10, "And behold, he shall be born of Mary, at Jerusalem which is the land of our forefathers, she being a virgin, a precious and chosen vessel, who shall be overshadowed and conceived by the Power of the Holy Ghost, and bring forth a son, yea, even the Son of God."

4. **The Book of Mormon is against the facts (which are now history) of this life.** In Luke 23:44 we read, "And it was now about the sixth hour, and a darkness came over all the earth until the ninth hour." All recognize this figures to three hours. In the Book of Mormon we read, "But behold, as I said unto you concerning another sign, a sign of his death, behold in that day that he shall suffer death the sun shall be darkened and refuse to give his light unto you and also the moon and the stars and there shall be no light upon the face of this land, even from the time that he shall suffer death for the space of **three days** to the time that he shall rise again from the dead." (Helaman 14:20).

5. **There is a contradiction within their own works and their practices.** 3 Nephi 18:8, Book of Mormon reads, "And it came to pass that when he said these words, he commanded his disciples that they should take of the wine of the cup and drink of it, and that they should also give unto the multitude that they might drink of it." Section 27:2, Doctrine and Covenants reads, "For behold, I say unto you, that it mattereth not what ye shall eat or what ye shall drink, when ye partake of the sacrament, if it so be that ye do it with an eye single to my glory." (Water is used instead of "wine of the cup" as an element in the Mormon worship).

6. **Another contradiction within their faith and practice is noted here.** Read Sections 124, 127 and 128, Doc-

trine and Covenants. It is clear in these sections that they teach and practice baptizing for the dead, yet the Book of Mormon, Alma 32:32-33 reads, "For behold this life is the time for men to prepare to meet God, yea, behold the day of this life is the day for men to perform their labors. And now, as I said unto you before, as ye have had so many witnesses, therefore, I beseech of you that you do not procrastinate the day of your repentance until the end; for after this day of life, which is given us to prepare for eternity, behold, if we do not improve our time while in this life, then cometh the night of darkness wherein there can be no labor performed."

The Authority for the Christian Science religion proves itself contradictory with the Scriptures to which it says it is the key.

1. **Science and Health with Key to the Scriptures proves contradictory to all science and health spiritually and physically.** Page 475, Line 28, reads, "Man is incapable of sin, sickness, death." This is against known facts which are recognized even by men who are not religious. Rather than being a key to the Scriptures it is a key to something foreign, for the Bible says in Romans 3:23 "For all have sinned" and again in 1 John 1:10 "If we say that we have not sinned, we make him a liar, and his word is not in us." Hebrews 9:27 states, "It is appointed unto men once to die, but after this the judgment." If a man cannot be sick, what did Paul mean in 2 Timothy 4:20 when he said, "Erastus abode at Corinth: but Trophimus have I left at Miletum sick?"

2. **Page 75, Lines 2-15 of Science and Health with Key to the Scriptures again contradicts what the master teacher Jesus said:** "Jesus said of Lazarus: 'Our friend Lazarus sleepeth; but I go, that I may awake him out of sleep.' Jesus restored Lazarus by the understanding that Lazarus had never died not by an admission that his body had died

and then lived again." Contrast this to John 11:14 "Then Jesus therefore said unto them **plainly, Lazarus is dead.**"

3. **Science and Health with Key to the Scriptures denies the facts and evidence that are recognized as history.** Page 44, Lines 28-29 state. "His disciples believed Jesus to be dead while he was hidden in the sepulchre whereas he was alive." Contrast this to Revelation 1:18 "I (meaning Jesus—IRS) am he that liveth, and was dead; and, behold, I am alive forevermore." Also read Matthew 28:1-10; Mark 16:1-9; Luke 24:1-2; John 20:12; 1 Corinthians 15:17.

4. **Science and Health with Key to the Scriptures denies what the God of Heaven has to say, yet they contend He is the guide.** Page 336, Line 10 "Immortal man was and is God's image or idea, even the infinite expression of infinite mind and immortal man is coexistent and coeternal with that mind." Contrast this to Genesis 1:27 "And God created man in his own image."

In reality, what we are doing here is comparing the Bible with other books. A similar investigation of all religious authorities will produce the same results. The promises of the Bible are consistent; no contradiction exists. It is consistent with science, archeology, common sense and has all the earmarks of the work of the Supreme Mind of God. All other books and creeds can be shown not to be the Word of God by similar reasoning. There are sixty-six books in the Bible, written by about forty writers over a period of about 1600 years, some of whom never saw each other and did not live to see the fulfillment of the prophecies about which they wrote—a masterpiece which the mind of man could not have accomplished.

Concerning the Modernist's and Evolutionist's Attitude

There are other groups of people who recognize that books other than the Bible are not the words of God, but also say they cannot be sure that the Bible is the final authoritative word of God. These people are represented

by the modernists and evolutionists, yet even their attitude cannot disprove the Bible to be the final authority.
Presumably the modernist and the evolutionist have investigated the Bible, and even though their conclusions
are far apart, neither of them will accept the Bible in its
entirety. The modernist does not deny the Scriptures out-
right, but believes the gospel for one age will not suit another age because of the need for progression—that you
cannot believe and obey the Bible in its entirety and accept modern science intelligently at the same time—that
such stories as Jonah and the whale are not believed to
actually have happened—the modernist would imply his
mind is better adapted to state in this age what is necessary for salvation than the minds of those that received
the revelation as recorded in the Bible. In answer to a
question from this writer, Harry Emerson Fosdick wrote
on November 9, 1955: "Modernism cannot be neatly de-
fined. The word covers varied opinions . . . Multitudes of
people earnestly desiring to be Christian were torn between their inherited theology on one side and their intelligent acceptance of modern science on the other . . .
In the late nineteenth and twentieth centuries the term
modernism arose. The modernists were those who over
against the fundamentalists claim that all truth is God's
truth; that the new knowledge and the Christian gospel
are not irreconcilable; one can be both an intelligent modern and a devout Christian; that we Christians are not
bound by ancient world views such as a flat and stationary
earth, creation in six days, etc.; and that the Bible is the
record of a progressive revelation of God's grace, culmina-
ting in Jesus Christ." There is conflict with the beliefs
of the modernists and the Bible. The Bible does not leave
room for additions nor subtractions. 1 Corinthians 4:6,
Revelation 22:18-19, 2 Timothy 3:16-17, 2 John 9. The
facts of science do not prove the Bible wrong, and you can
intelligently accept modern science and believe and obey

the Bible in its entirety at the same time. According to
Mr. Fosdick's statement, modernists would confuse the
truth of "creation in six days" as revealed in the Bible,
with an ancient view, not revealed in the Bible, of "a flat
and stationary earth." The Bible stands the supreme test
in making claims of truth—it reveals knowledge for all
minds in all ages to have—it takes the courage to tell the
world of all ages where man came from, why he is placed
upon the earth, what man is, and where he will go. God
breathed into man and he became a living soul—and God
breathed into the world a living gospel—the Bible. Actually, the modernist does not base his vague rejections of
the Scriptures upon knowledge, which he claims to possess,
but upon supposition. One modernist rejection is that hell
may not really be hell as described in the Bible. He has no
evidence that this is truth, but bases that belief upon a
supposed belief or understanding. There is certainly more
evidence to prove that there is a hell than there is to suppose there is not. The same Mind that said there would be
an eternal hell has proven in recorded history His vengeance and punishment upon those who choose not to follow Him. Those past facts and promises of hell to come,
and other future things are a result of the Supreme Mind
of God while the ideas contradicting the Bible are from
mere man.

**Not every Scripture or thought must be examined to
have faith in Jesus Christ.** An old sailor was asked by an
apprentice one day: "You must be awfully smart—do you
have to know every obstacle in this channel?" The sailor
replied: "No, just those that will cause trouble." We do
not have to know every word of God in order to obey His
Will, but we will never begin learning what we must do if
we do not begin an actual study of the Bible. Thus, as
soon as the individual admits the possibility that the Bible
is the Word of God, begin an actual study of it—continuing a study of it will produce faith (Romans 10:17). Don't

wait until you have won every argument in this connection. Work on the principle presented here, and in this type of study, as in any other, use the basic underlying principle of this entire book—allow the individual to read the passages from the Bible himself—don't quote them to him.

There is one exception to the courage of men in telling others from whence they came. The evolutionists will take up the dare of trying to tell man how he began, and will present their ideas concerning the possibilities of the source of man himself. The evolutionists differ greatly in their own field but they have the same basic tenants. They use mathematics, a system of counting cells and advancement, to support their claims. They choose to tell us that we "evolved" from one cell to a higher cell and then on higher, each bearing from the preceding lower accounting. I was studying with a man one time who contended this theory must be right. I listened patiently to his arguments and tried to overcome each one as he presented them. I felt that I was right in each instance, but the man would have a ready answer to try to show where I was wrong, then I would have an answer to try to prove he was wrong. The study stretched over several weeks' time and one day I was discussing the arguments with another man in the congregation. He said, "Ask him from where that first amoeba came." In our next study, I gave this question and the man had no answer. I did, and said, "Only the Bible is brave enough to venture the answer, 'In the beginning God created'." The man hung his head and told me he had been thinking for a long time that only the Word of God had the answer to questions such as this one. We continued our study, investigating the Word of God over a few more weeks and the man became firmly convinced and obeyed the gospel. Time, patience in study, much thought and prayer in your preparation of lessons, will aid you greatly in studies of this nature.

The following account came to me by way of bulletin, and I think it well worth your study. Brother Pat Hardeman, professor at Florida Christian College, is the compiler:

THE BIBLE ACCOUNT . . .

"And God said, Let us make man in our image, after our likeness . . . So God created man in his own image, in the image of God created he him; male and female created He them . . . And the Lord God formed man of the dust of the ground, and breathed into his nostrils the breath of life; and man became a living soul . . . In the day that God created man, in the likeness of God made he him; male and female created he them, and blessed them and called their name Adam." (Genesis 1:26, 27; 2:7; 5:1, 2).

(Note: Evolutionists criticise Christians for assuming so much about creation. . . Evolutionists do not even assume— they guess! As for me and mine, we will serve God!)

It is getting to be popular for a man to find a number of bones over any large area and from them draw a picture of the missing link. Hundreds have been invented.

EVOLUTION'S ACCOUNT . . .

"Man is descended from a quadruped, furnished with a tail and pointed ears, probably arborial in its habits, and an inhabitant of the Old World. This creature, if its whole structure had been examined by a naturalist, would have been classed among the Quadrumana, as surely as would the common and still more ancient progenitor of the Old and New World monkeys. The Quadrumana and all the higher mammals are probably derived from an ancient marsupial animal and this through a long line of diversified forms, either from some reptilelike or amphibianlike creature, and this again from some fishlike animal. In the dim obscurity of the past we can see that the early progenitor of the Vertebrata must have been an aquatic animal, provided with branchiae, with the two sexes united in the same individual." (Darwin's "Descent of Man." 2,372).

Behind every item in the universe is an intelligent cause. Nothing just happened. Someone has said that chances of drawing ten pennies (each numbered one to ten) one at a time in their numerical order is one to ten billion. Take a good watch, dismantle it and throw the pieces to the four winds. The chances of all those pieces coming together again and giving the correct time is impossible.

The same is true of the universe. No watch, no universe just happened. I am indebted to George DeHoff and his book **Why We Believe the Bible** for the two following illustrations which so clearly demonstrate this point. A story is told about an atheist who approached Benjamin Franklin and asked him who made the model he was displaying. This model demonstrated the proximity of the earth to the planets. Since Franklin knew what the man believed, he replied, "No one made it. It made itself, it just happened." "You're joking" the man told Franklin. "And so is the man who says the universe just happened," replied Franklin. Another story is told of an atheist who once said, "Show me your God. Let me see, hear, smell or taste him and I will believe." A Christian replied to him, "Show me your brains—let me see, hear, feel, smell or taste them and I will believe." The evolutionist, the modernist, the atheist—all cannot disprove the statements of the Bible—It will stand the test. Jesus said, "Heaven and earth shall pass away but my words shall never pass away," and certainly through wars, ignorance, burnings and definite efforts to destroy the Bible, in word or deed, it has come through and we have it today, as will be true in every age.

The Honest Questioner

Often honest people do not know whether or not to accept the Bible as the Word of God because they have not investigated. While writing this chapter a woman called me on the telephone and asked, "How do you know the Bible is the Word of God?" She was not rejecting it for any specific reason for she had no reason to eliminate it, but was afraid to say it was until she had knowledge of the proof. Sometimes this question is followed by, "Do we have any of the original manuscripts? I have heard that they do not exist." We must admit that not a single original manuscript exists today—at least none has been found.

If and when the originals are found, the text will prove
to be essentially what we have today. Why? Because too
much evidence exists to prove that these were preceded
by authoritative original manuscripts. The following
chart of catalogues listing the New and Old Testament
books by name is one example of the proofs. Manuscripts
must have existed in their day or else they would not have
been able to catalogue them on purpose or incidentally.
They must have existed continuously and then have been
lost. This is the equivalent of today's publications. Few
people ever see the manuscripts but they see many re-
prints. The same will be true of this publication. People
do not doubt that an original existed. It is possible that
you are reading a reprint and the manuscript of this work
is completely destroyed—but we never doubt that it existed. Note the dates overlap within this chart without a
single lapse of time. The chart carries us from the oldest known manuscript to those original manuscripts that
we do not have. These catalogues list the books known
as the Word of God at the time catalogued—both on purpose and incidentally as noted.

Identity of the catalogue or individual writing	Dates Recorded	Catalogue notations
Sinaitic Manuscript, "Every book is as old as its oldest existing copy." —McGarvey	300-350 AD	Contains most of the OT (Old Testament) (Sections lost by deterioration) and all of the NT (New Testament) as we now have it, plus two additional documents.
Council of Carthage	397 AD	Names all OT books and NT books. Gives council notes cataloguing books as we now have them—this is a step nearer to the original.

Athanasius— Bishop of Alexandria	326-373 AD	Lists all of the NT books and warns "some few of the weaker sort" to guard against the apocryphal books.
Cyril—Bishop of Jerusalem	315-380 AD	Lists all books of NT except Revelation in his instructions to candidates for baptism saying "Transgress not these bounds." It does not include the apocryphal books.
Eusebius—Bishop	270-340 AD	Lists every NT book as we have them today referring to these as "ancient authorities" —They had to be in existence long enough prior to this time to be noted as "ancient."
Origen—of Caesarea	185-254 AD	Names all OT books and NT books as we have them today. Writes incidentally on his commentaries of Joshua and Psalms.
Clement—of Alexandria	165-220 AD	He writes concerning all the NT books and quotes from all of them but four.
Tertullian—Bishop of Carthage	160-240 AD	In his debates with a heretic, Marcion, he named most of the books of the Bible as we have it today.
The Muratorian Canon	157 AD	Formal catalogue found in 1740 AD written by Pius, Bishop of Rome who was a possible contemporary of John (who died in 95 AD). This fragmentary writing lists most of the NT books. Missing sections due to deterioration probably contained those not noted, for that would complete the picture and make it agree as we have them.

| Marcion, found-er heretical party | 140 AD | While writing against the Bible he mentioned most of the books. |
| Ignatius— Bishop of Antioch | 37-108 AD | Quotes from the majority of the NT books. This is at the period of time they were written. |

This chart has been prepared from the material presented in a book entitled **Evidences of Christianity** by J. W. McGarvey, and published by the Standard Publishing Company of Cincinnati, Ohio.

Examine the Bible Itself

Up until now, we have examined and contrasted other works with the Bible, but we do not want to overlook an examination of the Bible itself. If I were wearing a suit and you should tell me it was nylon, I would not want to examine your suit to check that issue, but the suit in question. The Bible claims inspiration for itself. Read 2 Timothy 3:16, **"All Scripture** is given by inspiration of God," and 2 Peter 1:20-21, "That no prophecy of the Scripture is of any private interpretation. For the prophecy came not in old time by the will of man; but holy men of God spake as they were moved by the Holy Ghost." Examples of this are given in Exodus 4:12, "Now therefore, go, and I will be with thy mouth, and teach thee what thou shalt say," and in 2 Samuel 23:2, "The Spirit of the Lord spake by me and His word was in my tongue." Over 4,000 times the penmen of the Scriptures wrote saying, "Thus saith the Lord," "God spake" and "the Lord hath spoken it." If man could have, he would not have written the Bible and designated such to condemn him. Read Galatians 5:17-21 for a quick cataloguing of seventeen sins. The Bible moves with such great force in revealing secret things that only a Superior Mind could have guided. Isaiah 55:8-9 is clear on this point, "For my thoughts are not your thoughts, neither are your ways my ways, saith the Lord. For as the heavens are higher than the earth, so are my ways higher than your ways, and my thoughts than your thoughts."

Examination No. 1 **"Did the Bible reveal things long before they happened?"** This examination is not that which causes us to accept facts such as Methuselah was 969 years old, but rather whether events happened according to the will of God and by IIis power and guidance. As these points prove the positive, we can likewise prove God wrote the other lessons given in the Bible by the same power and guidance. The archaeologists, scientists, and historians, both Christian and non-Christian (and Jewish and Mohammedist) find themselves in agreement upon accepting facts. Likewise Protestant, Catholic and Jewish historians, scientists and archaeologists are in agreement with the facts, even though their application may be questioned. It takes courage to write history, yet God recorded history of His people, both good and bad. It is not distorted and one-sided.

1. 1 Timothy 4:1-3, "Now the Spirit speaketh expressly, that in the latter times some shall depart from the faith, giving heed to seducing spirits and doctrines of devils . . . **forbidding to marry,** and commanding to **abstain from meats,** which God hath created to be received with thanksgiving of them which believe and know the truth."

2. Ezekiel 26:12-14 tells of the destruction of Tyre. 350 years later we have recorded for us in secular history the literal fulfillment of this with Alexander the Great.

3. Joshua 6:26, "And Joshua adjured them at that time, saying, Cursed be the man before the Lord, that riseth up and buildeth this city Jericho; he shall lay the foundation thereof in his firstborn, and in his youngest son shall he set up the gates of it." Read 1 Kings 16:34 for the fulfillment of this statement.

4. Jeremiah 30:11, ". . . though I make a full end of all nations whither I have scattered thee, yet will I not make a full end of thee." We know from secular history of the destruction of all of the nations about Israel. The Jewish people stand scattered around the world as a testimony that He meant what He said. In history, no nation has been so blessed as the Jewish nation.

5. Isaiah 9:6, "For unto us a child is born, unto us a son is given; and the government shall be upon his shoulder; and his name shall be called Wonderful, Counsellor, The Mighty God, the everlasting Father, The Prince of Peace." Fulfilled in Jesus.

6. Micah 5:2, "But thou, Bethlehem Ephratah, though thou be little among the thousands of Judah, yet out of thee shall he come forth unto me that is to be ruler in Israel; whose goings forth have been from of old, from everlasting." See Matthew 2:1 for the fulfillment of this.

Examination No. 2, "Is the Bible in agreement with scientific knowledge, even though it is not a textbook on science?" While not all are scientists, scientific arguments (discernible facts) are helpful and convincing. While science as agreeing with the Bible does not teach how to be saved, it is convincing enough to show the knowledge of a Supreme Mind, and will help to thereby gain confidence in other areas upon which God chooses to speak, namely, the plan of salvation.

1. In AD 1735 Linnaeus is thought to have been the first to recognize the three divisions of mineral, vegetable and animal kingdoms, but God revealed it through Moses as recorded in the first chapter of Genesis.

2. Copernicus advanced a theory on planetary movement in AD 1543, but the Mind of God had already given it. (Job 38:31-32).

3. Modern shipbuilders understand that the best proportion for building ships is 3x5x30. In Genesis 6:15 we find that the ark was built on these dimen-

sions: 450 ft. long x 75 ft. wide x 45 ft. high. Compare any modern ship.

4. Franklin and Thomas Edison said that static electricity was caused by condensation of water but that thought was recorded many years prior to them in Jeremiah 10:13.

5. Matthew Fontaine Maury was supposed to have founded the study of oceanography and charted the lanes and paths of the sea which the ships follow today. He did this after he had studied the eighth Psalm and surmised that if God said there were paths in the sea, there must be.

6. Dr. Frank T. Shutt of the Canadian Department of Agriculture estimated the value of the action of snow and hail centrifuging through the air collecting nitrates, free ammonia and albuminoid ammonia. These are all valuable fertilizers, and Dr. Shutt estimates the value of an average winter's snow and hail at about fifteen dollars per acre to farm land. God revealed long ago in Job 38:22 there were treasures in the snow.

7. Hipparchus said in 150 B.C. that there were less than 3000 stars and Ptolemy said in AD 150 there were more than 3000 stars. After the invention of the telescope, men have said the stars are innumerable. Read Genesis 13:16; Genesis 15:5 and Jeremiah 33:22. God revealed that fact long before man admitted it.

8. Iron was forged just a few years, yet it is recorded in Genesis 4:22 that man worked with it long ago.

9. There is a known empty space in the North today and yet Job declared long ago, "He stretcheth out the North over the empty spaces and hangeth the earth up nothing." Job 26:17.

10. In recent years man has found fresh water springs at the floor of the salt water ocean. Read Job 38:16.

11. Columbus and a few others of his time believed the world to be round, not flat as it had always been thought to be. Then Magellan and his men sailed around the earth and proved it to be round. The

Author of Isaiah knew this and recorded in Isaiah 40:20, "It is God that sitteth upon the circle of the earth."

Science Research Bureau of Los Angeles, California has $500.00 reserved in a fund for some individual to prove that any science statement in the Bible is contradictory to scientific facts. This has been waiting to be collected for many years now.

(Most of the material in this examination was obtained from George W. DeHoff's book, **Why We Believe the Bible**).

Examination No. 3 **"Is the Bible Uninteresting?"** The Bible will remain uninteresting to those who do not desire to make it interesting to themselves. Science problems are not interesting to some simply because they do not make them interesting by wanting to understand them. Matthew 6:21, "For where your treasure is, there will your heart be also."

Examination No. 4 **"Is the Bible Difficult?"** It is true that one part may be more difficult than another. This does not mean that we should eliminate it for that reason. If we study and understand the simple parts we will come nearer to understanding the more difficult. If an individual considers algebra difficult, do we encourage him to not study it at all? If a problem is difficult for the doctor, do we discourage him from striving to solve it so he can determine a cure?

Examination No. 5 **"Is the Bible the same as the Roman Catholic Bible?"** The text of the Catholic Bible is translated very well. The scholars were honest to their scholarship. I have often said that an individual could read the text of the Catholic Bible and obey it and he would be a Christian, but he could read the footnotes and obey them and he would be a Catholic. W. Graham Scroggie points out in his book **Is the Bible the Word of God** that the New Testament writers knew the difference between the Old Testament writings and the Aprocrypha for they did not quote one single time from the Apocrypha, but did quote over 280 times from the Old Testament. (Page 55).

Examination No. 6 "Is it true that we do not know some of the penmen of certain books?" That is true—the book of Hebrews is a case in point, but the message is still binding. The Bible does not say "Except ye know who wrote every book of the Bible" but It does say "For if ye believe not that I am he, ye shall die in your sins." (John 8:24).

Examination No. 7 "Is it true that there are many variations in the manuscripts?" Some object to the adulterous woman account because it is not in two of the oldest manuscripts. Other old manuscripts do contain it, such as the Syrian and Latin and they are older dated manuscripts. Remember the scribes who made copies were human and may have left off some sections. The ravages of time caused others to be torn, burned, and become weather beaten. Philip Schaff wrote concerning variations, "Only about 400 of the 100,000 or 150,000 variations affect the sense. Again, not more than 50 are important for some reason or other; and of these 50 not one affects an article of faith or a precept of duty which is not abundantly sustained by other and undoubted passages or by the whole tenor of Scriptural teaching." The same problems exist in other writings. Copies of works contain variations; originals are not to be found, but we do have copies considering them authentic.

Examination No. 8 "Is it true that intelligent men reject the Bible?" As the world counts intelligence, yes; but it is equally true that some very intelligent men admit or have admitted the Bible is the Word of God. Here is a partial list of some of those men: Henry Ford, Winston Churchill, Woodrow Wilson, John Quincy Adams, Thomas Jefferson, George Washington, Abraham Lincoln, Spinoza, Thomas Decker, Daniel Webster, Thomas Paine, Ralph Waldo Emerson, Charles Dickens, Lord Byron, Rosseau, Shakespeare, and Robert E. Lee—many others of course.

Examination No. 9 "How can you accept the Bible when you have never seen any of the writings or writers?" We accept it upon faith, which is demanded of all by God. There is enough evidence in the Bible Itself to produce that faith if man will earnestly examine it. We accept other things by faith without half as much evidence. None of the men listed in Examination No. 8 have been seen by most men today, yet there is no doubt they lived and wrote and did the things for which they are famous. We accept the testimony of those who did see them and wrote about them. So do we of the Bible.

Examination No. 10 **"Is the Bible an enduring influence?"** All are seriously concerned about the world in which we live. None desire to live in a world completely bereft of the infuence of the gospel because it is for good. No philosophy or ideal has influenced as long and so much as the Bible. This should help especially with the ideal, ethical and moral minded. The Bible teaches us how to exist one with another.

Other examinations could proceed along the same line and each time the Bible proves true.

It is certainly true then that the psalmist was right when he wrote, guided by God: "The fool hath said in his heart there is no God." (Psalm 14:1). The eighth Psalm invites us to witness God Himself in and out of the Bible "When I consider thy heavens, the work of thy fingers, the moon and the stars" because "The heavens declare the glory of God; and the firmament showeth forth his handiwork." (Psalm 19:1). We need to learn the presence of God in everything. Psalm 139:8-10 reads, "If I ascend up into the heaven, thou art there; if I make my bed in hell, behold, thou art there. If I take the wings of the morning, and dwell in the uttermost parts of the sea, even there shall thy hand lead me." God has told us in Acts 17:28 "For in him we live and move, and have our being." Can a man doubt his very existence?

THE SCRIPTURES

INTRODUCTION

In this chapter we want to give the Scriptures that have worked most successfully. It is wise to always begin with the first Scripture and to cover all of the study regardless of the extent of the individual's knowledge. This allows you to cause him to say "yes" over and over again. It allows you the opportunity to refer back to things he has agreed upon previously when he disagrees. The application of the agreement on the previous principle can be referred to him at the time of the disagreement to show the inconsistency and to make an appeal for him to be consistent. In presenting the Scriptures in this section, it is assumed the person has accepted the Bible as the word of God. If the person accepts the Scriptures, it is unnecessary to present the information contained in the previous chapter. It is on that same basis that you should not present the side-track Scriptures unless needed. You may enlarge your own side-track Scriptures. If you leave the main track Scriptures for any reason at all (such as answering questions with other Scriptures), strive always to return to the main track. It is not the aim to cover everything in this section, but to show how to form a proper attitude in presenting the Bible.

A warning is necessary. Be as natural as possible. Do not be rigid, but weave yourself and the individual into the presentation. Use enthusiasm and confidence. Stock answers should not become a part of your natural life. Do not be afraid to say "I do not know." Have a small concordance (preferably in the back of at least one of the Bibles) and search with the individual, even guiding him in the use of it. List the Scriptures most frequently needed other than the main track and side-track Scriptures on one of the fly leaves of your Bible for easy reference.

It is wise to mark your Bible with the main track chain Scriptures. The chain of main track Scriptures is designed to cover the New Testament plan of salvation, the Bible way of worship, how to live the Christian life after baptism, and to point out error. These Scriptures are basical toward how to have eternal life and do not answer every religious problem, however, the purpose of this study is to enable you, as a personal winner of souls, to go into the person's home, sit down and study with him, and in one or a very few sessions show how he may begin the Christian life. They are also designed to assist you in helping the person with obedience at the close of the study. This is just the beginning and I in no wise advocate segregating these Scriptures as the only Scriptures on these subjects but these have worked most successfully for me and I pass them on to you. Study them yourself, study the context, familiarize yourself with the historical background and related Scriptures and thoughts and you will have a basis upon which to begin. In everything there must be a beginning and this is certainly the time for you now— BEGIN. Begin by marking the main track references in your Bible. No longer can you offer the excuse, "I can't remember or I can't find the Scriptures when I want them." For instance, the first reference should be Galatians 4:21-30. At the spot opposite that Scripture, write the next chain reference, Colossians 2:14, and then at Colossians 2:14 write the next reference, Hebrews 8:6-9 and so forth. Side-track Scriptures should be written at the bottom of the page of the Scripture that concludes that subject or at the end in the case of Scriptures to be used in final persuasion. Other Scriptures that you may need from time to time should be written on one of the fly leaves in your Bible. All emphasis points should be studied and presented naturally without notes. If you must, write the questions at the top of the page in pencil directly in the Bible.

Previously, it was suggested you take with you, if possible, Bibles that are alike in pagination, then as you ask the first question and state, "Let us look to the Bible for the answer"—you say where the Scripture is found and, if you use the Bibles alike and the prospect is having difficulty finding the reference, suggest the page number. In every instance, you turn to the reference also, but **please** let the person read the reference aloud himself. It will mean so much more to him. Then, also allow him to answer the question, using as many words from that particular Scripture as he can. The plea of this whole study is not to integrate man's ideas, but always to present the Bible.

After you have marked your Bible, and studied the emphasis and procedure, it might be wise to help you gain confidence and to more thoroughly familiarize yourself with the Scriptures and questions, to go over the whole process with someone who is a member of the church, who will listen attentively and make suggestions as you finish.

The narrative that we desire to weave into this study is "How to Have Eternal Life by Doing the Will of God." Now, look at the sample notes given in the chapter entitled "METHOD OF ACTUAL STUDY." These are the notes that you should strive to leave for further study. Remember, as you present the lesson, you sometimes need only bring to remembrance things already believed or sometimes to cause additional Bible knowledge and conviction. Sometimes we need to correct, but let us allow the Bible to do that in a proper way, so the person will see God's way and not our way. If we have presented the gospel properly, we can be almost sure the conviction will be forthcoming and the response certain. We could now say, "On your mark, get set, GO." GO even if you make a mistake for it is a bigger mistake not to GO. It is simple and you will gain confidence as you do more and more of this work.

THE SCRIPTURES

SIDE-TRACK SCRIPTURES

MAIN TRACK SCRIPTURES

EMPHASIS AND PROCEDURE

1. After all are seated and ready, suggest, "May we pray that God will guide our study?"

2. After the prayer, then say, "Since we cannot answer or study everything, may we study how we can have eternal life?"

3. "We cannot read every Scripture, but we can do the same as when we study geography. If we want to know what grows in Africa, we look under Africa. We do not look under Africa and say that the same things grow in America unless we compare and check the reading under America. Therefore, we will turn to several places where it is talking about how we may have eternal life."

4. "Since we believe the Bible to be the word of God, we need to see which part of the word of God we should follow—the Old Testament or New Testament. Let us look at the following chart and then check the Scriptures to see to which Testament we should go."

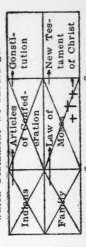

A. "As in the Civil rule we are not under two laws at the same time."
B. "The previous laws are fulfilled, not destroyed—just not binding."
C. "Illustration: Two people make a contract to build a house. Once finished, it cannot be revised. A new contract must be made in order to be binding."
   a. Mt. Sinai
   b. 52 days before Pentecost
   c. Pentecost
   x. fulfilled
D. Describe this chart as you prepare it.

5. "Now let us back this illustration up with the Scriptures. Remember, let us take our answers from God."

1. "What does one mother and son represent?"
2. "What does the other mother and son represent?"
3. "Which representation do we want?"
4. "What saith the Scriptures concerning Hagar and her son and their presentation?" Verse 30.
5. Chart the following while gaining the answers:

Galatians 4:21-31

21 Tell me, ye that desire to be under the law, do yo not hear the law? 22 For it is written, that Abraham had two sons, the one by a bondmaid, the other by a free woman. 23 But he who was of the bondwoman was born after the flesh; but he of the free woman was by promise. 24 Which things are an allegory; for these are the two covenants; the one from the mount Sinai, which gendereth to bondage, which is Agar. 25 For this Agar is mount Sinai in Arabia, and answereth to Jerusalem which now is, and

Colossians 2:14

—136—

is in bondage with her children. 26 But Jerusalem which is above is free, which is the mother of us all. 27 For it is written, Rejoice, thou barren that bearest not; break forth and cry, thou that travailest not: for the desolate hath many more children than she which hath a husband. 28 Now we, brethren, as Isaac was, are the children of promise. 29 But as then he that was born after the flesh persecuted him that was born after the Spirit, even so it is now. 30 Nevertheless what saith the Scripture? Cast out the bondwoman and her son: for the son of the bondwoman shall not be heir with the son of the free woman. 31 So then, brethren, we are not children of the bondwoman, but of the free.

Colossians 2:14

14 Blotting out the handwriting of ordinances that was against us, which was contrary to us, and took it out of the way, nailing it to his cross;

Hebrews 8:6-7

6 But now hath he obtained a more excellent ministry, by how much also he is the mediator of a better covenant, which was established upon better promises. 7 For if that first covenant had been faultless, then should no place have been sought for the second.

One son - Ishmael	One Son - Isaac
Mother - Hagar	Mother - Sarah
Represents one covenant - OL	Represents one covenant - NL
Source: Mt. Sinai	Source: Jerusalem
Bondage	Freedom
Not promised	Promised

Cast out which one?
See verse 30.

1. "Was the Old Law against them? Us?"
2. "What ended the Old Law? When?"
3. Remind: Take answer from the Scriptures—this builds up good training and ground work for the whole study.

1. "Do you see the idea of two covenants?"
2. "Do you see that one is better than the other? Which one?"
3. "Is the New Law the one we want to study?"

Romans 15:4

4 For whatsoever things were written aforetime were written for our learning, that we through patience and comfort of the Scriptures might have hope.

Romans 2:1-4
Hebrews 10:1-9
Galatians 3:15-24

1. "What value is the Old Testament to us then?"
2. "Illustration: We do not follow the laws of the Articles of Confederation, but we can learn much from them."

2 Timothy 3:16-17

16 All Scripture is given by inspiration of God, and is profitable for doctrine, for reproof, for correction, for instruction in righteousness: 17 That the man of God may be perfect, thoroughly furnished unto all good works.

John 20:30-31
1 Corinthians 4:6
2 John 9
Revelation 22:18-19

1. "Is the Bible (New Testament) complete?"

2 Peter 1:3

According as his divine power hath given unto us all things that pertain unto life and godliness, through the knowledge of him that hath called us to glory and virtue.

1. "Has God given us all that pertains to life and godliness?"

John 10:1

1 Verily, verily, I say unto you, He that entereth not by the door into the sheepfold, but climbeth up some other way, the same is a thief and a robber.

1. "If we try to go any other way to heaven do we sin?"

John 10:10

10 The thief cometh not, but for to steal, and to kill, and to destroy: I am come that they might have life, and that they might have it more abundantly.

Heaven our Goal
John 14:1-3

1. "Let us go to the complete New Testament and ask Jesus how we may enter Heaven."
2. "Why did the thief come?"
3. "Why did Jesus Christ come?"
4. "Is this the eternal life that we want?"

2 Peter 1:3   2 Timothy 3:16-17   John 10:1   John 10:10   John 14:6

John 14:6

6 Jesus saith unto him, I am the way, the truth, and the life: no man cometh unto the Father, but by me.

Matthew 7:21-23

21 Not every one that saith unto me, Lord, Lord, shall enter into the kingdom of heaven; but he that doeth the will of my Father which is in heaven. 22 Many will say to me in that day, Lord, Lord, have we not prophesied in thy name? and in thy name have cast out devils? and in thy name done many wonderful works? 23 And then will I profess unto them, I never knew you: depart from me, ye that work iniquity.

1. "Can anyone else give us this eternal life?"
2. "Does this eliminate me (my conscience)?"
3. "Does this eliminate your plan and the plan of Mary Baker Eddy? Roger Williams? the Pope? Joseph Smith? John Knox? The Wesley Brothers?" Point out these are leaders and founders of religious groups. Ask him if he would like to know the founder of any specific group.

1. "Will all who say Lord, Lord' (desire) enter the Kingdom of Heaven?" Just a Yes or No for the answer.
2. "Illustration: Next Sunday Baptists, Methodists, etc., and the church of Christ shall say 'Lord, Lord' — does that promise them eternal life?"
3. "Will Jesus send honest sincere people to hell who just do 'Many wonderful works'?" Just a Yes or No for the answer.
4. "Will Jesus send honest sincere people to hell?" Just a Yes or No answer.
5. "Illustration: There are good people in all churches—who can be a member of all to partake of the good and at the same time indulge in that which divides them?"
6. "How can we be sure then that we

can enter the Kingdom of Heaven?"
Take the exact words "DO HIS WILL"
out of verse 21.

7. "Illustration: A man approaches you and offers you a Cadillac and tells you he is the only man that can give it to you. You want it badly and ask how you can get it. He replies, 'Don't do just a few good things, but do my will?' What would you ask him next?' The answer should be "What is your will?'"

1. "How many will be in heaven? hell?"
2. "Where do we want to go?"

1. "How much of His will must we do?"
2. Instruction: Write on notes: "DO ALL HIS WILL."
3. "Let us continue our search through the complete New Testament to find out what is His will, because I am sure you do not want to do just part of it and miss heaven, do you?"

1. "What will cause us to keep his commandments?"

Matthew 7:13-14

13 Enter ye in at the strait gate: for wide is the gate, and broad is the way, that leadeth to destruction, and many there be which go in thereat: 14 Because strait is the gate, and narrow is the way, which leadeth unto life, and few there be that find it.

Matthew 28:18-20

18 And Jesus came and spake unto them, saying, All power is given unto me in heaven and in earth. 19 Go ye therefore, and teach all nations, baptizing them in the name of the Father, and of the Son, and of the Holy Ghost: 20 Teaching them to observe all things whatsoever I have commanded you: and lo, I am with you alway, even unto the end of the world. Amen.

John 14:15

15 If ye love me, keep my commandments.

John 3:16

16 For God so loved the world, that he gave his only begotten Son, that whosoever believeth in him should not perish, but have everlasting life.

John 8:24

24 I said therefore unto you, that ye shall die in your sins: for if ye believe not that I am he, ye shall die in your sins.

Hebrews 11:6

6 But without faith it is impossible to please him: for he that cometh to God must believe that he is, and that he is a rewarder of them that diligently seek him.

REPENTANCE:

Luke 13:3

3 I tell you, Nay: but, except ye repent, ye shall all likewise perish.

Acts 17:30

30 And the times of this ignorance God winked at; but now commandeth all men every where to repent:

2 Corinthians 7:10

10 For godly sorrow worketh repentance to salvation not to be repented of:

John 3:18
John 2:19
Source of Faith:
Romans 10:17

1. "What is His will?"
2. Write down "Belief" under "DO ALL HIS WILL." Belief equals understanding. The Bible constantly bestows upon human mind the ability to understand IT.

1. "Can I still go to heaven if I fail to believe?"

1. "Is there any way to still please God without faith?"
2. "Do you have any questions on believing?"
3. "Do you enjoy studying this way?"

1. "What is His will here?"
2. Write down "Repent" under "DO ALL HIS WILL."
3. "Can I still go to heaven without repentance?"

1. "Are any exempted?"
2. Illustration: One woman read this passage and said she was exempted because it read "all men." This word refers to all mankind.

1. "What is repentance or how do I repent?"

Illustration: Infant ⟶ GOD

Devil ⟵

but the sorrow of the world worketh death.

Acts 3:19

19 Repent ye therefore, and be converted, that your s ins may be blotted out, when the times of refreshing shall come from the presence of the Lord;

CONFESSION:
Matthew 10:32-33

32 Whosoever therefore shall confess me before men, him will I confess also before my Father which is in heaven. 33 But whosoever shall deny me before men, him will I also deny before my Father which is in heaven.

Romans 10:9-10

9 That if thou shalt confess with thy mouth the Lord Jesus, and shalt believe in thine heart that God hath raised him from the dead, thou shalt be saved. 10 For with the heart man believeth unto righteousness; and with the mouth confession is made unto salvation.

Matthew 16:15-17

15 He saith unto them, But whom say ye that I am? 16 And Simon Peter answered and said, Thou art the Christ,

3. "What kind of sorrow? **Godly** is an adverb telling what kind of sorrow."

1. "What is repentance or how do I repent?"
2. "Are there any questions on repentance?"
3. Do not go on until he understands this clearly.
4. Again emphasize the joy and the ease in reading directly from the Bible.

1. "What is His will here?"
2. "Where is this confession made?"
3. Illustration: Note places where not made such as behind black cloth, etc.
4. "Who is to be confessed?"
5. "Are sins to be confessed here?"
6. "Can I still enter heaven without confessing?"
7. Write down "Confess" under "DO ALL HIS WILL."

1. "How do I confess?"
2. Illustration: Some say, "Sign a card or questionnaire — wear a handkerchief — confess at mourner's benches — in prayer tent — touch the television set or the radio. All of these are wrong. aren't they?

1. "Do we have a Bible example for a confession?"
2. "If we confess just this will we be

the Son of the living God. 17 And Jesus answered and said unto him, Blessed art thou, Simon Bar-jona: for flesh and blood hath not revealed it unto thee, but my Father which is in heaven.

Acts 8:37

Acts 8:37 (Not in 1901 translation)

37 And Philip said, If thou believest with all thine heart, thou mayest. And he answered and said, I believe that Jesus Christ is the Son of God.

united with Peter and all others who make the same confession?"

3. "Did his confession please Jesus?"

1. "Do we have another Bible example of a confession?"
2. "Would the lack of the confession and belief made known in the confession have hindered the eunuch in his baptism?"
3. "Are there any questions on the confession? This is clear, isn't it?"
4. Do not proceed until all these subjects presented till now are understood.

BAPTISM:

Matthew 28:18-19

18 And Jesus came and spake unto them, saying, All power is given unto me in heaven and in earth. 19 Go ye therefore, and teach all nations, baptizing them in the name of the Father, and of the Son, and of the Holy Ghost:

1. "What else do we learn here is His will?"
2. Write "Baptism" on the notes under "DO ALL HIS WILL."
3. "Can infants be taught so as to be subject to baptism?"
4. "In what name (or authority) should you be baptized?"
5. "What is the extent of Jesus' authority?"
6. "Does that leave any authority for anyone else upon this earth?"

Mark 10:13-16

15 And he said unto them, Go ye into all the world, and preach the gospel to

1. "Does baptism have anything to do with being saved?"
2. "Why did He not say 'those not bap-

every creature. 16 He that believeth and is baptized shall be saved; but he that believeth not shall be damned.

Acts 2:37-47

37 Now when they heard this, they were pricked in their heart, and said unto Peter and to the rest of the apostles, Men and brethren, what shall we do? 38 Then Peter said unto them, Repent, and be baptized every one of you in the name of Jesus Christ for the remission of sins, and ye shall receive the gift of the Holy Ghost. 39 For the promise is unto you, and to your children, and to all that are afar off, even as many as the Lord our God shall call. 40 And with many other words did he testify and exhort, saying, Save yourselves from this untoward generation. 41 Then they that gladly received his word were baptized: and the same day there were added unto them about three thousand souls. 42 And they continued steadfastly in the apostles' doctrine and fellowship, and in breaking of bread, and in prayers. 43 And fear came upon every soul: and many wonders and signs were done by the apostles. 44 And all that believed were together, and had all things common; 45 And sold their possessions and goods, and parted them to all men, as every man had need. 46 And they, continuing

Acts 8:35-39

tized shall be damned' in just those words'" Note he did not have to be- cause you cannot baptize an unbe- liever; he is damned, just as one who is not baptized is damned.

1. "Is being 'pricked in the heart' the same or equal to repentance?"
2. "What 'shall' they 'do'?"
3. "Why be baptized?"
4. "Did they quibble and try to alter the fact and mode of baptism?"
5. "Did they join a church?"
6. "Who added them to the church?"
7. "Where were the 'saved' unsaved placed?"
8. "Do you think any unsaved were placed in the church? Why were they not added to the church also?"

daily with one accord in the temple, and breaking bread from house to house, did eat their meat with gladness and singleness of heart, 47 Praising God, and having favor with all the people. And the Lord added to the church daily such as should be saved.

Acts 8:35-39

35 Then Philip opened his mouth, and began at the same Scripture, and preached unto him Jesus. 36 And as they went on their way, they came unto a certain water: and the eunuch said, See, here is water; what doth hinder me to be baptized? 37 And Philip said, If thou believest with all thine heart, thou mayest. And he answered and said, I believe that Jesus Christ is the Son of God. 38 And he commanded the chariot to stand still: and they went down both into the water, both Philip and the eunuch; and he baptized him. 39 And when they were come up out of the water, the Spirit of the Lord caught away Philip, that the eunuch saw him no more: and he went on his way rejoicing.

Ephesians 4:5

5 One Lord, one faith, one baptism,

1. "Since the denominational world is divided on baptism, let us see how he was baptized."
2. "Was he sprinkled? Poured? Immersed?"
3. "In what element was he immersed?"
4. Illustration: Often it is wise to read this saying "he went into a pitcher of water and came out of it." This shows the error of pouring and sprinkling because it does not read that way.
5. Illustration: Baptism is objected to because you cannot be sure who was baptized here. If the long-haired man and the short-haired barber went into a barber shop, and he got his hair cut, who got the haircut? You reply: "The one who needed it". The same is true here. "Who needed to be baptized?"

1. "The Bible shows how many Lords?"
2. "The Bible shows how many baptisms?"
3. "Can all these be right: immersion— pouring — sprinkling — Holy Spirit — none?"

Romans 6:3-4

3 Know ye not, that so many of us as were baptized into Jesus Christ were baptized into his death? 4 Therefore we are buried with him by baptism into death: that like as Christ was raised up from the dead by the glory of the Father, even so we also should walk in newness of life.

Galatians 3:27

27 For as many of you as have been baptized into Christ have put on Christ.

1 Corinthians 12:13

13 For by one Spirit are we all baptized into one body, whether we be Jews or Gentiles, whether we be bond or free; and have been all made to drink into one Spirit.

Colossians 2:12

Acts 2:41
Acts 16:33
Acts 16:15
Acts 22:16
Acts 10:48
John 3:23
Not of Holy Spirit—for
  it was a promise.
Acts 1:4
Acts 18:24-28
Acts 19:1-5

—145—

1. "How was Paul baptized?"
2. "Is this the one baptism?"
3. "How should we be baptized?"
4. "Illustration: Imagine a family pet dog died. The wife and children demanded that it be buried directly under the kitchen window. Since we have heard a lot about substitution for burial as sprinkling and pouring, we conclude it will work in burying animals, so we sprinkle some sand on it. How long do we think it will be until we are called to redo our job of burying the pet? How long if we pour some dirt on it?"

1. "Into what were they baptized?"
2. "Do we conclude that this is the way to get into Christ?"

1. "Into how many bodies (churches) were they baptized?"
2. "Does this show how to enter Christ and His kingdom?"
3. "Are there any questions on baptism?"
4. "Is it clear and wonderful to understand?"

DO ALL IN HIS NAME:

Colossians 3:17

17 And whatsoever ye do in word or deed, do all in the name of the Lord Jesus, giving thanks to God and the Father by him.

Acts 4:12
Philippians 2; 9
Ephesians 1:22-23

1. "What else is the Will or God?"
2. "How much must be done IN HIS NAME?"
3. "Will any name do?"
4. Write "DO ALL IN HIS NAME," under "DO ALL HIS WILL."

John 17:11

11 And now I am no more in the world, but these are in the world, and I come to thee. Holy Father, keep through thine own name those whom thou hast given me, that they may be one, as we are.

1. "Does Jesus want us to be more than ONE?"
2. "What name was given to God's Son?" Note that it was not Luther, Wesley, Knox, etc.

1 Corinthians 1:10-13

10 Now I beseech you, brethren, by the name of our Lord Jesus Christ, that ye all speak the same thing, and that there be no divisions among you; but that ye be perfectly joined together in the same mind and in the same judgment. 11 For it hath been declared unto me of you, my brethren, by them which are of the house of Chloe, that there are contentions among you. 12 Now this I say, that every one of you saith, I am of Paul; and I of Apollos; and I of Cephas; and I of Christ. 13 Is Christ divided? was Paul crucified for you? or were ye baptized in the name of Paul?

Signs of false teachers
Ephesians 5:6-11
2 John 9
Galatians 1:8-9
Matthew 7:15
Matthew 15:9

1. "How does Jesus want us to speak?"
2. "How can we speak the 'SAME THING' when one says one thing and one another, as:
   a. Baptism does not save us and
   b. Baptism does NOW save us.
   or a. Any name will do and
   b. Only the name of Jesus will do?"
3. Illustration:

Mind of God revealed in Bible

Baptists ---- Church of Christ

John 17:11   1 Cor. 1:10-13   1 Corinthians 3:3-6

"The broken lines represent not speaking the same thing and the solid line means 'SAME SPEECH'. Does the Baptist Church and the church of Christ speak the same thing? This demonstrates how we can test who is speaking the same as the mind of God."

4. Put verses 12 and 13 into modern language, pointing out that this was division in that day, as sectarianism and denominationalism is today! "Now this I say, that every one of you saith, I am of Paul (Luther); and I of Apollos (John Knox); and I of Cephas (the Pope); and I of Christ. Is Christ divided? Was Paul (Luther) crucified for you? or were ye baptized in the name of Paul (Luther)?"

1. "Are we carnal (sinful—worldly) when one says, 'I am of Paul (Luther); and another, I am of Apollos (John Knox)?"

1 Corinthians 3:3-6

3 For ye are yet carnal: for whereas there is among you envying and strife, and divisions, are ye not carnal, and walk as men? 4 For while one saith I am of Paul; and another, I am of Apollos; are ye not carnal? 5 Who then is Paul, and who is Apollos, but ministers by whom ye believed, even as the Lord gave to every man? 6 I have planted, Apollos watered; but God gave the increase.

Colossians 1:18

Colossians 1:18

18 And he is the head of the body, the church: who is the beginning, the first-born from the dead; that in all things he might have the preeminence.

Ephesians 4:4

4 There is one body, and one Spirit, even as ye are called in one hope of your calling;

Matthew 16:18

18 And I say also unto thee, That thou art Peter, and upon this rock I will build my church; and the gates of hell shall not prevail against it.

Acts 2:47

47 Praising God, and having favor with all the people. And the Lord added to the church daily such as should be saved.

1. The aim in this section is to show the difference between the denominations and the true church.
2. "Who is the head of the church?"
3. "How many churches? Bodies?"
4. Show how church and body are equal.

1. "How many spirits?"
2. "How many bodies? churches?"

1. "How many churches? Bodies?"
2. "Whose church did Christ say He would establish?"
3. "Illustration: Whose name does a man want the girl he marries to wear?"
4. "Illustration: If a man establishes a grocery store and puts his name on it, can you expect to place your name on it also?"

1. "To what church do you think Jesus added these people?" Especially con-sider—none of these existed:

Nazarene—1907
Methodist—1729
Lutheran—1517
Baptist—1522
Presbyterian—1536
Mormon—1830
Catholic—606
 (First Pope) 606
Christian—1739

Acts 20:28

28 Take heed therefore unto yourselves, and to all the flock, over the which the Holy Ghost hath made you overseers, to feed the church of God, which he hath purchased with his own blood.

Romans 16:16

16 Salute one another with a holy kiss. The churches of Christ salute you.

1. "Who purchased the church?"

2. Illustration: "Often this reference is used to prove Church of God is correct name to wear. That is right—but not the denomination wearing that name. Several denominations wear the name "Church of Christ," then add another phrase, as Christian Scientist, Mormon, some Lutheran, and some Christian churches."

Illustration to help understand: "If you have a Cadillac car and that is what you want, you expect it to wear the right name and to have the right motor (workings). If we put a Chevrolet motor in it—would it be a pure Cadillac? Let us have the right name and the right motor (workings)." Compliment the prospect for recognizing the right name (if he does)—we need to have the right motor and have the courage to wear just the name authorized in Colossians 3:17.

1. "What church do we read about here?"

2. "Sometimes it is argued that the use of the word "churches" is plural and thus includes all of the denominations. How could they all be the true church when they speak different things? The word church is used singularly and plurally. One church at one location and collectively was known as the church. Imagine a chain

1 Corinthians 3:11
Colossians 1:13
Isaiah 2:2-4
1 Chronicles 17:11-12
Isaiah 62:1-5
Isaiah 56:5
Ephesians 5:23-24

—149—

of grocery stores. In one location the store is known as XYZ and the same store located over an area would still be known as the XYZ stores. That is singular and plural use, and they are one and the same—take one out and you would not have the ABC store or the DEF store in name or practice."

3. "We use other terms singularly and plurally. Mr. A may have one house in Dallas, one house in Ft. Worth and another in Austin. When we talk about Mrs. A's house at Ft. Worth we might say, 'Mr. A's house' but when we talk of Mr. A's houses at the other locations we might say, 'Mr. A's houses'. We understand who is the owner in each place. The houses belonging to someone else are not referred to as Mr A's houses. The church is in Ft. Worth and Dallas and Austin. One congregation is the church of Christ or all are churches of Christ, but they are alike in name and doctrine."

4. "Is there any question over what name to wear and what church we are to fellowship?"

1. "It is possible to claim a Bible name and still be wrong, such as Nazarene and Christian Church?"

2. "Let us illustrate: Who equals Christians?"

MISAPPLICATION OF THE SCRIPTURE
Acts 11:26

26 And when he had found him, he brought him unto Antioch. And it came to pass, that a whole year they assembled themsleves with the church, and

Eph. 1:3

taught much people. And the disciples were called Christians first in Antioch.

IS THE CHURCH IMPORTANT:
Ephesians 1:3
3 Blessed be the God and Father of our Lord Jesus Christ, who hath blessed us with all spiritual blessings in heavenly places in Christ:

LORD'S SUPPER:
Matthew 26:26-29
26 And as they were eating, Jesus took bread, and blessed it, and brake it, and gave it to the disciples, and said, Take eat; this is my body. 27 And he took the cup, and gave thanks, and gave it to them, saying, Drink ye all of it; 28 For

Luke 22:19-20   Matt. 26:26-28

Ask:
    What? equals Christian
    (He should fill in Disciple.)
    "To call it the Christian Church is to call it the Disciples' Church and since Disciples and Brethren are equal terms, it opens the door for the Brethren Church and Luther would call himself a Disciple, Brother, Christian, and thus open the door for the Lutheran Church, and so on. Christ never sold His Church to the disciples or a group of disciples. Christian is the proper term for the individual, but the individuals belong to the body of obedient believers which Christ Himself adds to His Body, His Church."
3. "We do not want to be guilty of this, do we?"

Acts 2:47
1 Corinthians 12:13

1. "Is the church important?"
2. "If 'ALL' blessings are 'in Christ' (church) are there any out of Christ?"

1. "What else is His will?"
2. "What elements are authorized?"
3. "Would we think of using steak or cake on the Lord's Table?"
    (Refer to this later if he wants to add the mechanical instruments of music.)

—151—

this is my blood of the new testament, which is shed for many for the remission of sins. 29 But I say unto you, I will not drink henceforth of this fruit of the vine, until that day when I drink it new with you in my Father's kingdom.

Luke 22:19-20

19 And he took bread, and gave thanks, and brake it, and gave unto them, saying, This is my body which is given for you: this do in remembrance of me. 20 Likewise also the cup after supper, saying, This cup is the new testament in my blood, which is shed for you.

John 6:53-54

53 Then Jesus said unto them, Verily, verily, I say unto you, Except ye eat the flesh of the Son of man, and drink his blood, ye have no life in you. 54 Whoso eateth my flesh, and drinketh my blood, hath eternal life; and I will raise him up at the last day.

Acts 20:7

7 And upon the first day of the week, when the disciples came together to break bread, Paul preached unto them, ready to depart on the morrow; and continued his speech until midnight.

Might point out special religious holidays unscriptural. Galatians 4:10-11

4. Write "PARTAKE OF THE LORD'S SUPPER" under "DO ALL HIS WILL" on notes.

1. "Are all to partake of it?"
2. "Illustration: Some use water, some give only bread to the communicant —is this right?"

1. "Can I still go to heaven if I fall to partake of the Lord's Supper?"

1. "How often shall we partake of it?"
2. Illustration: Point out that some partake of the Lord's Supper at various times: once a month (first Sunday of month)—once a quarter (first Sunday of quarter)—some weak Christians (C&E—Christmas and Easter).
3. "If you lived under the Old Law and

John 6:53-54   Acts 20:7   1 Cor. 16:1-2

CONTRIBUTION:
1 Corinthians 16:1-2

1 Now concerning the collection for the saints, as I have given order to the churches of Galatia, even so do ye .2 Upon the first day of the week let every one of you lay by him in store, as God hath prospered him, that there be no gatherings when I come.

1 Corinthians 9:1-7
1 Timothy 5:17-18
2 Corinthians 12:13

Read, 'Remember to keep the Sabbath holy', how many Sabbaths would you keep holy? What about the Lord's Supper in the New Law?" See Exodus 20:8.

1. "What else is the will of the Lord here?"
2. "When should we give of our means?"
3. "How much should we give?"
4. "Is the giving under the New Law the same as tithing under the Old Law?"
5. Show the New Law superior over the Old Law. "It is possible to obey the New Law or God would have made it otherwise—therefore, we only cheat ourselves if we cheat God." Show where the New Law is centered upon the word GROWTH. Therefore, suggest that we grow with gradual increases in giving.
6. Write "GIVE OF OUR MEANS" under "DO ALL HIS WILL" in the notes.
7. "Are there any questions on contribution?"

Be sure to not state a specific amount. Give some examples if he asks. "We should strive to grow and work it out with God as witness. The elders should know all about our spiritual lives—therefore, giving is not a secret matter and all else open—all should be open. Talk this over with the elders where you will worship."

ATTENDANCE:

Hebrews 10:25

25 Not forsaking the assembling of ourselves together, as the manner of some is; but exhorting one another: and so much the more, as ye see the day approaching.

Hebrews 13:17
1 Corinthians 16:1-2
Revelation 1:10
Acts 20:7

1. "What else is the will of the Lord here?"
2. Write "ASSEMBLE WITH THE SAINTS" under "DO ALL HIS WILL" in the notes.
3. "May we miss the assembly? Which ones yes and which ones no? Are all assemblies included here?"
4. Often people want to know the authority for the mid-week services. Hebrews 13:17 is the authority if the elders set it as a time to be fed.
5. "Are there any questions on attendance?"

STUDY:

Acts 2:42

42 And they continued steadfastly in the apostles' doctrine and fellowship, and in breaking of bread, and in prayers.

1. "What is the will of the Lord that the early Christians continued in here?"
2. Write "CONTINUE IN APOSTLES' DOCTRINE" (STUDY) under "DO ALL HIS WILL."

2 Timothy 2:15

15 Study to show thyself approved unto God, a workman that needeth not to be ashamed, rightly dividing the word of truth.

1. "What are we to study?"
2. "Since we cannot cover everything now in this study or many similar periods—we need to constantly study, don't we?"

Philippians 1:9

9 And this I pray, that your love may abound yet more and more in knowledge and in judgment;

Hebrews 5:11-14

1. "Do you see the need for growth?"
2. "Are there any questions on STUDY and GROWTH?"

PRAYER:

1 Thessalonians 5:17

17 Pray without ceasing.

James 4:3
1 Timothy 2:5

1. "What else is His will here?"
2. Explain "pray without ceasing."
3. Write "PRAY" under "DO ALL HIS WILL," in the notes.
4. "Are there any questions on prayer?"

PRAISE:

Ephesians 5:19

19 Speaking to yourselves in psalms and hymns and spiritual songs, singing and making melody in your heart to the Lord;

1. "What else is His will here?"
2. "How many melodies are used here?"
3. Write "PRAISE" under "DO ALL HIS WILL," in the notes.
4. "How are we to make this melody?"
5. "Do you see the absence of the instrument here?"

Colossians 3:16

16 Let the word of Christ dwell in you richly in all wisdom; teaching and admonishing one another in psalms and hymns and spiritual songs, singing with grace in your hearts to the Lord.

Hebrews 13:15
James 5:13
1 Corinthians 14:15
Hebrews 2:12

1. "Do you see that will stated again here?"
2. "What are we to do when we sing? —praise, speak, admonish, teach." Give him the following chart and have him work it:

	Voice	Instrument
Speak	Can	Cannot
Admonish	Can	Cannot
Teach	Can	Cannot

(Chart used by permission of Fred Walker)

Revelation 22:18-19

18 For I testify unto every man that heareth the words of the prophecy of this book, If any man shall add unto these things, God shall add unto him the plagues that are written in this book:
19 And if any man shall take away from

1. "Can we add anything here or anywhere else?"
2. "Can we add to the Lord's Table?"
3. Illustration: "Often we hear that the Bible does not say NOT to have the instrument. This Scripture says NOT

the words of the book of this prophecy, God shall take away his part out of the book of life, and out of the holy city, and from the things which are written in this book.

have anything not authorized and certainly it is NOT authorized."

4. "Do you want the plagues promised here added to you?"

1 Corinthians 4:6
(Use 1901 translation, if available)

6 And these things, brethren, I have in a figure transferred to myself and to Apollos for your sakes; that ye might learn in us not to think of men above that which is written, that no one of you be puffed up for one against another.

2 John 9
The Bible complete. 2 Timothy 3:16-17. Same principle in Old Testament. Deuteronomy 4:2

1. "Are we permitted to go beyond the things written?"

Galatians 1:6-9

6 I marvel that ye are so soon removed from him that called you into the grace of Christ unto another gospel: 7 Which is not another; but there be some that trouble you, and would pervert the gospel of Christ. 8 But though we, or an angel from heaven, preach any other gospel unto you than that which we have preached unto you, let him be accursed. 9 As we said before, so say I now again, If any man preach any other gospel unto you than that ye have received, let him be accursed.

1. "Can we have any gospel other than that delivered here?"

2. "Illustration: You agree to have a house built and the contract specifies brick, and you leave town while the contractor builds it. When you return, he tries to have you accept the house sight unseen. You refuse and investigate and then you see why—it is made out of corrugated tin—would you accept it? No, why not? Because it is not according to the contract."

3. "Do you want to build your hopes upon things not in the Covenant?"

4. "Are there any questions on the way to praise God?"

THE CHRISTIAN LIFE:
Romans 12:1

1 I beseech you therefore, brethren, by the mercies of God, that ye present your

1 Peter 4:16

1. "What else is the will of the Lord?"
2. Write that we are to "SERVE" and

Galatians 1:6-9

Romans 12:1

bodies a living sacrifice, holy, acceptable unto God, which is your reasonable service.

Titus 2:11-14

11 For the grace of God that bringeth salvation hath appeared to all men, 12 Teaching us that, denying ungodliness and worldly lusts, we should live soberly, righteously, and godly, in this present world; 13 Looking for that blessed hope, and the glorious appearing of the great God and our Saviour Jesus Christ; 14 Who gave himself for us, that he might redeem us from all iniquity, and purify unto himself a peculiar people, zealous of good works.

Revelation 2:10

10 Fear none of those things which thou shalt suffer: behold, the devil shall cast some of you into prison, that ye may be tried; and ye shall have tribulation ten days: be thou faithful unto death, and I will give thee a crown of life.

Matthew 24:12-13

"SACRIFICE" under "DO ALL HIS WILL" in the notes.

3. Point out here that service is to come from us in order to please God.

1. "What else is His will here?"
2. Write the following in the notes under "DO ALL HIS WILL":
   a. Receive instruction
   b. Deny ungodliness
   c. Deny worldly lusts
   d. Live soberly
   e. Live godly
   f. Zealous for good works
3. "Of course, you know all of these generally, but a continued study will teach us specifically."
4. "We do not have to give up anything except the unscriptural."
5. "Are there any questions you have on living the Christian life?"

1. "How long are we to live the Christian life?"

James 4:17

17 Therefore to him that knoweth to do good, and doeth it not, to him it is sin.

1 Timothy 2:4
Hebrews 4:7
Revelation 22:7
Revelation 3:20
Not told just to pray but to OBEY
John 9:31
1 Peter 1:22
John 3:36
Acts 16:28-33
Conscience not always right
Acts 26:9-11
1 Timothy 1:15
Acts 23:1
1 Timothy 1:12-16
Not told to wait
Acts 2:41-47
Acts 8:36-39
Acts 16:33
Acts 22:16
Almost is but to fail
Acts 26:28
Proverbs 27:1
Hebrews 3:15
2 Corinthians 6:2
James 4:13-14

1. "Before we read this, I want you to recognize the truth here and answer the question I have to ask you regarding this Scripture, as honestly as you know how."

2. "Will it do me any good to learn to do these things and not do them?"

3. "Would you like to do what you have learned here in this study?"

4. If the answer is yes, ask if he would like to do them that night, or next Sunday or Wednesday (you gauge the best question here).

5. If he knows but does not say yes, pesuade him with the side-track Scriptures and these illustrations:

"What if you have a car that the gas tank on it holds ten gallons—you have filled it yourself and know this to be a surety. You go to a service station and tell the attendant to fill it up. He runs the register back, fills the tank and the meter registers twenty gallons. You rebel and he shows you the meter reading. You tell him it is wrong—he goes to the rear of the station and brings back a United States certified five gallon measuring can. Then you run the meter back to zero, fill the can and the meter registers ten gallons, showing it to be wrong. Do you expect him to change that meter and if so, when? What do you think the Lord expects us to do when we know we are wrong?"

"Last year an airplane just a few degrees off its course crashed into a mountain near my home. The pilot wasn't far off, just a few degrees, but he crashed. Do you want to miss heaven by just a few degrees?"

"When Noah and his family went into the ark and God closed the door were the people who were ten feet from the ark just as lost as those ten miles from the ark?"

6. If the prospect does not understand something, review: "Do you understand belief? Repentance? Confession? Baptism? What name to wear? How to Praise God? How to be faithful unto death?" If the answer is yes one by one, ask what stands in the way and then use some of the solutions suggested near the end of the chapter entitled "CLOSING."

1. Ask, "If you love the Lord. what should you do?"

—159—

John 14:15

15 If ye love me, keep my commandments.

Scriptures for Restoration

Often, elders and preachers call upon delinquent members of the church to make an appeal to them to return to their first love. It is a sad thing when Christians need to be asked to return to something that should demand all their love—Jesus—He loved us enough to die for us. It is a sadder thing when elders and preachers do not go or do go but unprepared. All of the principles involved in this book can apply in the case of restoration, only bringing to the delinquent's remembrance things applicable to his sin. It is always wise to state the reason you came. It is always wise to name the sin and to show him from the Bible the Scriptures dealing in that sin. This is part of the work of the church. First and foremost, the church has the responsibility to "make known the manifold wisdom of God" (Ephesians 1:3). Too often, we think this relates only to the effort of teaching and baptizing people. In making known the wisdom of God, we should strive to carry out all that God has commanded. "Teaching them to observe all things whatsoever I commanded you." Matthew 28:20. This teaching comes after baptism. God's people should put forth such teaching and admonition as to cause Christians to grow. To strengthen the brethren is a work of the Lord. When God's children do stray, it becomes the work of the followers of God to restore them to their first love. Galatians 6:1. Stronger Christians can often assist in doing the work of "supporting the weak" (1 Thessalonians 5:14) by saying to them, "I want you to go to heaven with me—won't you return to your first love—I am praying that you will." We cannot be shy about this matter because it is the work of the Lord, and if we are genuinely interested in the souls of men, even in delinquent souls, we will want to take the time and effort to talk with them and to pray for them. The following series of Scriptures may be followed in much the same fashion as prior to baptism.

It is suggested that you mark these Scriptures in your Bible with different colored ink or pencil than the other series, then there will be no chance of becoming mixed up on your chain series. Cause the delinquent person to read the Scripture if you can, if not, then read to him.

MAIN TRACK SCRIPTURES

Hebrews 12:4-11

4 Ye have not yet resisted unto blood, striving against sin. 5 And ye have forgotten the exhortation which speaketh unto you as unto children, My son, despise not thou the chastening of the Lord, nor faint when thou art rebuked of him: 6 For whom the Lord loveth he chasteneth, and scourgeth every son whom he receiveth. 7 If ye endure chastening, God dealeth with you as with sons; for what son is he whom the father chasteneth not? 8 But if ye be without chastisement, whereof all are partakers, then are ye bastards, and not sons. 9 Furthermore, we have had fathers of our flesh which corrected us, and we gave them reverence: shall we not much rather be in subjection unto the Father of spirits, and live? 10 For they verily for a few days chastened us after their own pleasure; but he for our profit, that we might be partakers of his holiness. 11 Now no chastening for the present seemeth to be joyous, but grievous: nevertheless, afterward it yieldeth the peaceable fruit of righteousness unto them which are exercised thereby.

EMPHASIS AND PROCEDURE

1. Tell him that you have come to talk to him about his soul.
2. "How is a son to regard the chastening of the Lord?"
3. "Who does the Lord chastize?" "We love you also and want to bring these things to your remembrance."
4. "How does all chastening seem for the present? After awhile?"

1 Corinthians 13

1 Though I speak with the tongues of men and of angels, and have not charity, I am become as sounding brass or a tinkling cymbal.

1. "Our attitude is that of this reading in coming to you."
2. "May we pray concerning our attitude in this period of guidance?" Then pray.

1 Corinthians 16:13-14

2 And though I have the gift of prophecy, and understand all mysteries, and all knowledge; and though I have all faith, so that I could remove mountains, a n d have not charity, I am nothing. 3 And though I bestow all my goods to feed the poor, and though I give my body to be burned, and have not charity, it profiteth me nothing. 4 Charity suffereth long, and is kind; charity envieth not; charity vaunteth not itself, is not puffed up, 5 Doth not behave itself unseemly, seeketh not her own, is not easily provoked, thinketh no evil; 6 Rejoiceth not in iniquity, but rejoiceth in the truth; 7 Beareth all things, believeth all things, hopeth all things, endureth all things. 8 Charity never faileth: but whether there be prophecies, they shall fail; whether there be tongues, they shall cease; whether there be knowledge, it shall vanish away. 9 For we know in part, and we prophesy in part. 10 But when that which is perfect is come, then that which is in part shall be done away. 11 When I was a child, I spake as a child, I understood as a child, I thought as a child: but when I became a man, I put away childish things. 12 For now we see through a glass, darkly; but then face to face: now I know in part; but then shall I know even as I am known. 13 And now abideth faith, hope, charity, these three; but the greatest of these is charity.

1 Corinthians 16:13-14

Col. 3:12-14

13 Watch ye, stand fast in the faith, quit you like men, be strong. 14 Let all your things be done with charity.

1. "How are Christians to conduct themselves after baptism?"
2. "How are we to do this period of study?"

Colossians 3:12-14

12 Put on therefore, as the elect of God, holy and beloved, bowels of mercies, kindness, humbleness of mind, meekness, longsuffering; 13 Forbearing one another, and forgiving one another, if any man have a quarrel against any: even as Christ forgave you, so also do ye. 14 And above all these things put on charity, which is the bond of perfectness.

1. "What kind of heart should we have?"
2. "What are we to do for each other? That is our attitude in coming—wanting to forgive and forbear."

John 13:34-35

34 A new commandment I give unto you, That ye love one another; as I have loved you, that ye also love one another. 35 By this shall all men know that ye are my disciples, if ye have love one to another.

1. "What is the new commandment?"
2. "How shall we all know we love one another?"
3. "Even in this rebuke and correction we want love to be manifested."

John 10:10

10 The thief cometh not, but for to steal, and to kill, and to destroy: I am come that they might have life, and that they might have it more abundantly.

1. "We want to review what Jesus did for us."
2. "Why did Jesus come into the world?"
3. "Do you want to go to heaven? Have that abundant life?"

John 14:6

6 Jesus saith unto him, I am the way, the truth, and the life: no man cometh unto the Father, but by me.

1. "Can anyone else give us the Eternal Life?"
2. "What about the way we conduct our lives—are we to have the approval of the Way (Jesus)?"

Matthew 7:21-23

21 Not every one that saith unto me Lord, Lord, shall enter into the kingdom of heaven; but he that doeth the will of my Father which is in heaven. 22 Many will say to me in that day, Lord, Lord, have we not prophesied in thy name? and in thy name have cast out devils? and in thy name done many wonderful works? 23 And then will I profess unto them, I never knew you: depart from me, ye that work iniquity.

1. "How may you and I have this Eternal Life?"
2. "May we enter heaven after we have done many wonderful works, if we have not done all His Will?"

Margin notes: John 13:34-35 · John 10:10 · John 14:6 · Matt. 7:21-23 · Matthew 7:13-14

Matthew 7:13-14

13 Enter ye in at the strait gate: for wide is the gate, and broad is the way, that leadeth to destruction, and many there be which go in thereat: 14 Because strait is the gate, and narrow is the way, which leadeth unto life, and few there be that find it.

1. "How many shall go to heaven? Hell?"
2. "Which number do we want be in?"

Titus 2:11-14

11 For the grace of God that bringeth salvation hath appeared to all men, 12 Teaching us that, denying ungodliness and worldly lusts, we should live soberly, righteously, and godly, in this present world; 13 Looking for that blessed hope, and the glorious appearing of the great God and our Saviour Jesus Christ; 14 Who gave himself for us, that he might redeem us from all iniquity, and purify unto himself a peculiar people, zealous of good works. 15 These things speak, and exhort, and rebuke with all authority. Let no man despise thee.

1. "The Scriptures are good to us to the intent that we can know what to do by their instruction—is that right?"
2. "What are we to deny? How are we to live?"

Romans 12:1

1 I beseech you therefore, brethren, by the mercies of God, that ye present your bodies a living sacrifice, holy, acceptable unto God, which is your reasonable service.

1. "What kind of a life are we to live?"
2. "Is the life you are now living sacrificing and serving?"

Then study the Scriptures pertaining to the actual sin or sins of the delinquent person with whom you are studying.

John 14:15

15 If ye love me, keep my commandments.

1. "Do you love the Lord enough to keep the positive commandments and leave undone those things that displease him?"

Revelation 2:5

5 Remember therefore from whence thou art fallen, and repent, and do the first works; or else I will come quickly, and will remove thy candlestick out of his place, except thou repent.

1. "What is told us here we must do if we have fallen?"

Acts 8:22

22 Repent therefore of this thy wickedness, and pray God, if perhaps the thought of thine heart may be forgiven thee.

1. "Does the Lord give us something to do here?"
2. "Is it an impossible thing?"

James 5:16

16 Confess your faults one to another, and pray one for another, that ye may be healed. The effectual fervent prayer of a righteous man availeth much.

1. "Do you see what we must do here?"
2. "We want to help you to have that 'effectual fervent prayer of a righteous man'."

James 4:17

17 Therefore to him that knoweth to do good, and doeth it not, to him it is sin.

1. "Will it do you any good to know these things and do them not?"
2. Go to here, if possible, on the first visit, then offer these suggestions:
   a. "May we pray for your restoration and change of life now and announce to the congregation this activity and change next Sunday (or next meeting time)?"
   b. "Would you prefer doing this next Sunday (or next meeting time)?"

If no response is shown to these Scriptures, we list below Scriptures to be used in following visits—in extreme cases and only as the elders approve:

Hebrews 13:17

17 Obey them that have the rule over you, and submit yourselves: for they watch for your souls, as they that must give account, that they may do it with joy, and not with grief: for that is unprofitable for you.

1. "Do you know your relationship to the elders and the elders' relationship to you?"
2. "We have a duty to do that is God's idea and not ours."

Acts 8:22

James 5:16

James 4:17

Hebrews 13:17

Romans 12:8

Phil. 3:15-16

Romans 12:8

8 Or he that exhorteth, on
exhortation: he that giveth,
let him do it with simplicity;
he that ruleth, with dili-
gence; he that showeth mer-
cy, with cheerfulness.

1. "How are the elders to rule?"

Matthew 28:18-20

Philippians 3:15-16

15 Let us therefore, as
many as be perfect, be thus
minded: and if in any thing
ye be otherwise minded,
God shall reveal even this unto
you. 16 Nevertheless, where-
to we have already attained,
let us walk by the same rule,
let us mind the same thing.

1. "Do we have a different rule
guiding us — both elders and
those subject to them?"

Galatians 6:1

Matthew 28:18-20

18 And Jesus came and
spake unto them, saying, All
power is given unto me in
heaven and in earth. 19 Go
ye therefore, and teach all
nations, baptizing them in
the name of the Father, and
of the Son, and of the Holy
Ghost: 20 Teaching them to
observe all things whatsoever I have commanded you:
and lo, I am with you alway,
even unto the end of the
world. Amen.

1. "What is the elders' responsibility toward the latter part of
the Great Commission?"
2. "What is every Christian's responsibility toward the latter
part of the Great Commission?"

James 5:19-20

Galatians 6:1

1 Brethren, if a man be
overtaken in a fault, ye
which are spiritual, restore
such a one in the spirit of
meekness; considering thyself, lest thou also be tempted.

1. "What is the responsibility of
those who are not overtaken by
trespass toward those who are?
That is the responsibility that
we feel toward you."

1 Thessalonians 5:14

James 5:19-20

19 Brethren, if any of you
do err from the truth, and
one convert him; 20 Let him
know, that he which con-
verteth the sinner from the
error of his way shall save
a soul from death, and shall
hide a multitude of sins.

1. "What happens if we can save
a sinner from the error of his
way?"
2. "We would be sinning if we
did not come and reason with
you, wouldn't we?"

1 Thessalonians 5:14

14 Now we exhort you, brethren, warn them that are unruly, comfort the feeble-minded, support the weak, be patient toward all men.

1. "This is God's instruction to us."

2 Timothy 3:16

16 All Scripture is given by inspiration of God, and is profitable for doctrine, for reproof, for correction, for instruction in righteousness:

1. "What will correct us? Are we supposed to use the Scriptures for correction? It corrects me (or us) as well as you. Not my opinions nor yours."

2 Timothy 4:2

2 Preach the word; be instant in season, out of season; reprove, rebuke, exhort with all longsuffering and doctrine.

1. "Are we to reprove and rebuke each other?"

Matthew 5:23-24

23 Therefore if thou bring thy gift to the altar, and there rememberest that thy brother hath aught against thee; 24 Leave there thy gift before the altar, and go thy way; first be reconciled to thy brother, and then come and offer thy gift.

1. Those going should offer in a humble way to correct if they have contributed in any way.

1 Corinthians 5:6-8

6 Your glorying is not good. Know ye not that a little leaven leaveneth the whole lump? 7 Purge out therefore the old leaven, that ye may be a new lump, as ye are unleavened. For even Christ our passover is sacrificed for us: 8 Therefore let us keep the feast, not with old leaven, neither with the leaven of malice and wickedness; but with the unleavened bread of sincerity and truth.

1. "Since this sin is of leavening influence not only to you, your family, friends, loved ones, but to the church, and community, we pray that you would make a change and remove it."

Marginal references (left edge, top to bottom): 2 Tim. 3:16 — 2 Tim. 4:2 — Matt. 5:23-24 — 1 Corinthians 5:6-8 — Matthew 18:15-20

Matthew 18:15-20

15 Moreover if thy brother shall trespass against thee, go and tell him his fault between thee and him alone: if he shall hear thee, thou hast gained thy brother. 16 But if he will not hear thee, then take with thee one or two more, that in the mouth of two or three witnesses every word may be established. 17 And if he shall neglect to hear them, tell it unto the church: but if he neglect to hear the church, let him be unto thee as a heathen man and a publican. 18 Verily I say unto you, Whatsoever ye shall bind on earth shall be bound in heaven; and whatsoever ye shall loose on earth shall be loosed in heaven. 19 Again I say unto you, That if two of you shall agree on earth as touching any thing that they shall ask, it shall be done for them of my Father which is in heaven. 20 For where two or three are gathered together in my name there am I in the midst of them.

Titus 3:10

1. "Again, please note the procedure that we must follow."
2. "We will attempt to give you every opportunity and follow the Bible."
3. "We hope that you see the error of your way and correct because you do not know if you will live until we can see you at least two more times—think of the souls you might influence between now and then, even if you do live."

Titus 3:10

10 A man that is a heretic, after the first and second admonition, reject;

1 Cor. 5:9-11

1. "Note after these several visits what must happen."

1 Corinthians 5:9-11

9 I wrote you in an epistle not to company with fornicators: 10 Yet not altogether with the fornicators of this world, or with the covetous, or extortioners, or with idolaters; for then must ye needs go out of the

2 Thessalonians 3:6

1. "With whom are Christians to have no company?" Point out that even though their sin may not be listed, the same principle applies since that sin is contrary to God's law (I t should have already been pointed out as wrong).

world. 11 But now I have written unto you not to keep company, if any man that is called a brother be a fornicator, or covetous, or an idolater, or a railer, or a drunkard, or an extortioner; with such a one, no, not to eat.

2 Thessalonians 3:6

1 Timothy 5:20

6 Now we command you, brethren, in the name of our Lord Jesus Christ, that ye withdraw yourselves from every brother that walketh disorderly, and not after the traditions which he received of us.

1. "What does God tell the faithful to do towards them that 'walk disorderly.' Can you feel ill toward us if we do just that? Remember we hope you do not continue disorderly."

1 Timothy 5:20

Eph. 5:10-11

20 Them that sin rebuke before all, that others also may fear.

1. "If you refuse to turn from your sin, where are you to be rebuked for your sin? Why?

Ephesians 5:10-11

Romans 16:17

10 Proving what is acceptable unto the Lord. 11 And have no fellowship with the unfruitful works of darkness, but rather reprove them.

1. "What should we do if you do not change according to the Scriptures?"

Romans 16:17

Acts 5:1-11

17 Now I beseech you, brethren, mark them which cause divisions and offenses contrary to the doctrine which ye have learned; and avoid them.

1. "What are we to do toward those doing things contrary to the doctrine?"
2. "Do you want us to do that? If you do not change, we will have no other alternative."

Acts 5:1-11

Revelation 2:5

1 But a certain man named Ananias, with Sapphira his wife, sold a possession, 2 And kept back part of the price, his wife also being privy to it, and brought a certain part, and laid it at the apostles' feet. 3 But Pe-

1. "Notice the wrath of God toward those in the church who did not do His will."
2. "Do you want that type of punishment, but forever?" (Give Scriptures on hell if necessary)
3. "Your sin may not be the same listed here, but in principle you

ter said, Ananias, why hath Satan filled thine heart to lie to the Holy Ghost, and to keep back part of the price of the land? 4 While it remained, was it not thine own? and after it was sold, was it not in thine own power? why has thou conceived this thing in thine heart? thou hast not lied unto men, but unto God. 5 And Ananias hearing these words fell down, and gave up the ghost: and great fear came on all them that heard these things. 6 And the young men arose, wound him up, and carried him out, and buried him. 7 And it was about the space of three hours after, when his wife, not knowing what was done, came in. 8 And Peter answered unto her, Tell me whether ye sold the land for so much? And she said, Yea, for so much. 9 Then Peter said unto her, How is it that ye have agreed together to tempt the Spirit of the Lord? behold, the feet of them which have buried thy husband are at the door, and shall carry thee out. 10 Then fell she down straightway at his feet, and yielded up the ghost: and the young men came in, and found her dead, and, carrying her forth, buried her by her husband. 11 And great fear came upon all the church, and upon as many as heard these things.

Revelation 2:5

5 Remember therefore from whence thou art fallen, and repent, and do the first works; or else I will come unto thee quickly, and will remove thy candlestick out of his place, except thou repent.

Acts 8:22

have not complied with God's commands." Point out that it is not you bringing judgment on them, but the revealed Word of God.

1. "What are we to do if we fall?"

James 5:16

Acts 8:22

22 Repent therefore of this thy wickedness, and pray God, if perhaps the thought of thine heart may be forgiven thee.

1. "When is your wickedness forgiven you?"

James 4:17

James 5:16

16 Confess your faults one to another, and pray one for another, that ye may be healed. The effectual fervent prayer of a righteous man availeth much.

1. "What are we told to do here?"

1 John 1:9

James 4:17

17 Therefore to him that knoweth to do good, and doeth it not, to him it is sin.

1. "What is the sin listed here?"

1 Pet. 4:18

1 John 1:9

9 If we confess our sins, he is faithful and just to forgive us our sins, and to cleanse us from all unrighteousness.

1. "What are we told to do here?"
2. "What is God's promise to us in this verse?"
3. "Is there any unrighteousness from which God will n o t cleanse you?"

END

1 Peter 4:18

18 And if the righteous scarcely be saved, where shall the ungodly and the sinner appear?

1. If they say they want to go to heaven, then point out that the righteous shall scarcely b e saved, don't they want to try to be among that number?
2. If they say they do not want to go to heaven — after several visits and emphasis on these Scriptures and others appropriate, then tell them the elders' decision and the date of withdrawal so they will have one more chance.
3. Again ask, "May we pray for your restoration and change of life now and announce to the congregation this activity and change next Sunday (or next meeting time)?"
   or
   "Would you prefer doing this next Sunday (or next meeting time)?"

FOLLOW UP

The Necessity of Follow Up

It is a must that we follow up after baptism, whether the individual is converted privately or publicly. Often people object to private study periods saying, "They do not know enough." Honestly, answer this question, "If an individual studies what is presented in the chapter on Scriptures, and understands and believes that, don't you think he knows enough to obey the gospel, and don't you think he will be judged thereby if he does not do so?" Then after baptism, if newborn babes begin and continue a steady, systematic study of the gospel, there is little danger of them falling by the wayside. If we fail to teach after baptism as admonished in the last section of the great commission as given in Matthew 28:18-20, we have sinned in this regard. A good enthusiastic follow-up program will help in this regard. We are suggesting several things that can be done relative to starting a follow-up program. There are no doubt many others. Let us work and improve ourselves by constantly studying the Bible and encouraging others to do so.

The new convert mortality rate is larger than it should be because of the stronger not taking care of the weaker. Recently in our city a baby, one year old, drank kerosene and died from it. Surely that mother must have said to herself, "I could have kept that kerosene out of his reach." When a newborn babe in Christ attends all the services for a season, then gradually becomes negligent, do you ask, "Have I done all I could to encourage and teach him?" Many times the babe has the zeal, yet little knowledge, and discovers he has done things he should not have done or has left undone things he should have done. Without continued encouragement and strengthening, he may wander away and become lost in due time. We fail to visit him, fail to encourage him, fail to teach him and thus we help him become lost. Someone has said that one-half of all baptized are lost within five years from the time of baptism. That rate may be high, but all of us should be alarmed if even one strays, and all of us can remember and place in our minds some who would fit into this category. Brethren, something is wrong if we can teach prospects and baptize them, but yet we cannot continue teaching them so they can become strong members of the church.

In Hebrews 5:12-14 we discover at least two classes of people in the Kingdom. The "babe" without experience, whose diet is milk, and those who are of "full age," whose food is strong meat. All individuals in the Kingdom are not of full age. Also along the line from milk to meat are varying degrees of individuals trying to get well and strong. The church is like a hospital full of individuals trying to get well and grow strong. There would be no need for the hospital if all could be strong of themselves, and thus there would be no need for Jesus' death and the Kingdom if all could be strong of themselves. However, we are weak by ourselves, but become stronger with God's help. As we become stronger Christians, we are to help the weaker Christians, to "bear their infirmities" (Romans 15:1).

When an individual is baptized, he should be made to realize that he is not a full grown Christian. When an individual is placed in the Army, he is not a General immediately. Even so, in the Kingdom of God, a person who has just obeyed the gospel is a newborn babe, and with an attitude of love in trying to help and assist, and not just to show that he is the low man on the totem pole, we should help him to realize he is just beginning the Christian life and to offer assistance in studying the Bible to grow stronger. The attitude is often this: Tom and Jane are wonderful individuals, all they have to do is be baptized—they live such good moral lives they wouldn't have to change a thing. This is erroneous. It is true many will not have to change as much as others, but baptism is not all they must do. Too often, individuals are swept right into the church as elders, deacons, teachers, etc. Their responsibilities are great and they are not able to bear the load, and after awhile they drift back to the way of the world—true, a child of God once, but lost and the last state is worse than never knowing. When an individual is baptized, the elders, the deacons, the preacher or some Christian should sit down and with an open Bible outline how to "be faithful until death," having now begun the Christian life. Whatever program we use, let us make it work and cease having to work so hard trying to save the saved that go astray because of lack of feeding and guidance and knowledge. One of the following programs might be chosen, or various ones used. These are discussed and explained more fully in the following pages, and of course they are all suggestions and may be varied:

1. Welcome letter

2. Welcome envelope

3. Be sure they have a Bible (Determine from family record)

4. New convert's class

5. Elders' program

6. Deacons' program

7. Alphabetical program

8. Zone program

9. Send literature or books (either one time or regularly). (Some listed in Bibliography).

A WELCOME LETTER

October 18, 1955

Dear Sister GHI:
789 Lancester
Albuquerque, New Mexico

Dear Sister GHI:

Welcome to the family of God! By your obedience last Sunday to the commands of our Saviour, you have been born into the family of God, and we want you to know that the saints meeting at this address are rejoicing with you.

We are enclosing a family record, together with a stamped, self-addressed return envelope. Please complete the record and return it to us at your earliest convenience. Please note on the family record whether you have a Bible or not.

You will soon receive a copy of the _____ which the elders are having sent to each home monthly.

You are invited to study in the new converts' class. It meets Sunday morning at 9:45 in Room 3 and Brother Cox, an elder, is the teacher.

Sincerely in Christ

Ivan R. Stewart

Similar letters should be sent after restoration and identification.

WELCOME ENVELOPE

This idea was derived from the many courtesy wagons that visit newcomers to a city and give them an envelope containing advertisements of the various merchants. A large brown envelope may be used and partially prepared ahead of time. Listed below are suggestions to go into the envelope. It might also be mailed or delivered in person, and of course, they are much more effective if delivered in person with a short visit. The following items are suggested for the new convert—variations of these items will suit newcomers to the city:

Bibliography of books to help in Bible study.

List of Church papers.

Latest Church bulletin or Newsletter.

Tracts—especially "Is Church Attendance Necessary?" by Hobbs

Membership list.

Telephone numbers of preacher, assistant, song leader, elders, deacons, church secretary.

Outlines of any important lessons being taught.

Questionnaire (if not included in welcome letter).

Enrollment blank for correspondence course if offered.

List of books in library if you have one.

List of radio and television programs.

Picture of building if available.

Enrollment forms for Bible School.

Lessons on how to understand the Bible, etc.

New Converts' Class

A class for new converts will assist greatly. This may be conducted through the mail in the form of a Bible Correspondence Course. It may be conducted on Sunday morning or evening or even during the week. It is wise that an elder conduct this class. A course "Foundation Facts For Salvation" by this author could be used as a text as well as Brother Brownlow's book "Why I am a member of the church of Christ." This class should be limited in time, preferably no longer than a six months' period. Do not endeavor to study the whole Bible, but do begin the foundation well. Subjects such as these should be discussed:

1. The necessity of study.

2. How to study the Bible.

3. How to pray properly.

4. How to remain faithful until death.

5. How to worship properly.

6. How to partake of the Lord's Supper properly.

7. Responsibility toward the eldership.

8. How to help win others to Christ.

9. Questions from the class.

10. The work of the church (emphasize local work).

The best way to form and continue a new converts' class is by invitation of the elders. The following letter is self-explanatory:

CHURCH OF CHRIST - Netherwood Park
5101 Indian School Road, N.E.
Albuquerque, New Mexico
October 3, 1955

Dear Mr. ABC:

You are invited to become a member of the New Converts' Class which will convene next Sunday morning, October 9, at 9:45 a.m. All who have been baptized in recent months are invited to be your classmates. One of the elders, Brother Virgil Cox, will be the teacher.

This class is being started to help fulfil the latter part of the Great Commission, as recorded in Matthew 28:18-20 "Go ye therefore, and teach all nations, baptizing them in the name of the Father, and of the Son, and of the Holy Ghost: **teaching them to observe all things whatsoever I have commanded you.**" Paul said in Romans 6:4 that after baptism we are to "walk in newness of life." It is this new life and a continued faithfulness in it that we desire that you have.

This class will study all things that pertain to the growth of the newborn babe such as: How to study the Bible, How to pray publicly and privately, How to give properly, church attendance, Relationships to the elders and others in the church, etc. You may have another subject that you would like to discuss. If so, please mention it.

When this class is completed, you may attend one of the other adult classes. At that time, others who have obeyed the gospel will then take your place in the New Converts' Class.

As elders of the church, we feel it our duty to feed you the Word of God and this is one of the ways that we feel we can best serve you. We will be looking forward to your presence and participation in the class. Please consider this a personal invitation.

We pray your faithfulness and love for the Lord will grow more and more in all knowledge of the Lord.

Sincerely in Christ,
The Elders:
Virgil Cox
Erroll Gay
A. L. Gower
Wayne Stell

The Elders' Program

The elders should have a program that helps them in feeding the flock. Too many times, the elders do not even know who they are feeding. If the elders are not already acquainted with individuals who respond to the invitation, it is best to become acquainted with them at the time of their response. If they do this, they will soon know all that they are feeding. Elders should know the names and general location in which they live, something about their spiritual status, and other things about the ones for whom they are watching. The Family Record will assist in this matter—a sample of it is in the chapter entitled The Office Procedure.

The elders could announce themselves available for feeding the flock. The elders need to announce to the membership constantly that they are available for counselling. One step further might be gained by having a class entitled "Bible Questions Answered." This class would have no set enrollment and no set curriculum, except the Bible. The elders announce the location of this class as other classes. As the people have questions they may leave their regular class and consult with the eldership. They may study with the elders one Sunday or several and then return to their regular class.

The elders need to see that every home is visited. This should be their instructions to the preacher as well as to themselves. They need to set aside a definite time, a day a week if possible and certainly no less than a day each month, to visit in the homes of the members and especially the new converts. This visitation can be enlarged upon by the suggested deacons' program in this chapter or the membership visitation program mentioned in the chapter on The Office Procedure. Set a definite night, monthly or even quarterly, for the membership visitation program and you will find more will participate that night. It will also inspire them to visit at intervals between the dates set for regular visitation nights.

The Deacons' Program

The elders need to assign every deacon a definite job assignment. These assignments may be individual or duplicated or several deacons may be assigned to one task. Some suggested assignments are mimeographing, library, flowers, inside and outside building duties, ushering, purchasing materials, helping in Bible School, bookkeeping, Lord's Supper, counting contribution and many others, and they should be considered for the follow up program. This suggested program could be guided through one elder or the assignment given to one deacon. It is suggested that the program be designed to indoctrinate the new converts relating to fellowship and a closer tie to the family of God. The aim is to concentrate on them for one year, and then they can in turn help others.

1. Visit —   2 weeks   after baptism — Deacon No. 1

2. Visit —   1 month   after baptism — Deacon No. 2

3. Visit —   3 months after baptism — Deacon No. 1

4. Visit —   6 months after baptism — Deacon No. 2

5. Visit —   9 months after baptism — Deacon No. 1

6. Visit — 12 months after baptism — Deacons No. 1
                                                        and 2

Each visit should deal with a definite plea. Example: Visit number one may deal with welcome and encouragement and answering any questions that they may have—if you have a class for new converts, give a personal invitation at this time. Visit number two may deal with questions, "Are you studying and praying?" Visit number three may deal with "Are you giving properly and visiting others?" Visit number four may deal with "Do you know who the elders are and what your relationship is to them?" Visit number five may deal with "In what parts of the worship would you like to help?" Of course this will show up on the family record, but after several months their desires should be greater due to more familiarity and growth. Visit number six may deal with "continued faithfulness until death." Of course the elders may have a definite aim or program to get over to the people and they can make assignments to the deacons accordingly. Each visit should be informal and the problem presented gradually, making them feel welcome and helping them to grow on the personal basis of instruction. These visits may take only twenty to thirty minutes or longer, depending upon the interest and problems raised. These of course are merely suggestive and you can work out a similar program or alter this one.

Alphabetical Program

The following page contains instructions which are self-explanatory and can help to inaugurate a personal work program using the alphabetical method. These assignments may be done by the elders, given to deacons or others of the congregation. The form is typed so as to be cut, folded and placed in the front of small uniform books with a list of those to be checked. This system has many advantages over the zone system. You do not have to constantly notify of additions or deletions—the leaders take them from the news in the church bulletin, and add or delete as necessary. It eliminates a complicated office system such as map with pins, etc. The alphabetical list should be divided so that no more than 15-18 families will be assigned to each zone leader. It is better to have about 10 families in each group.

PERSONAL WORK PROGRAM

Church of Christ—Netherwood Park
5101 Indian School Road, N.E.
Albuquerque, N. M., Phone: 5-9967

_____Coordinator

_____Phone

This book assigned to the Worker marked with an *.

A - C _____

D - G _____

H - L _____

M - N _____

O - R _____

S - Z _____

1. As a personal worker, keep an up-to-date roll. Add and delete information as it appears in the Newsletter.

2. If some on your list are not present at least once on Sunday —on Monday mail a Newsletter to them with note: "We missed you yesterday." Pick up exact number needed to be mailed on Sunday evening.

3. If absent 2 weeks in a row, either call or visit them personally plus mailing the Newsletter.

4. Give information about sickness or other problems to the elders or the preacher. (Do not allow yourself to be "floored" at some of the problems of Christians.)

5. If you cannot visit someone who needs visiting, speak to the coordinator.

6. If you must be absent, please be sure that somebody else makes the check for you and should you not be able to properly serve in this capacity at any time—let the Coordinator know ahead of time.

7. If you need stamps (2c), procure them from_____ here at the building from time to time. Be sure to keep a supply ahead.

8. Know those on your list—visit to become acquainted if need be.

9. Visit everyone on your list at least once every _____ months.

10. Visit every person who answers the invitation in your alphabet category.

11. Should your list grow too large by additions for you please report it.

12. Make any suggestions you have from time to time.

13. REMEMBER: If just one Personal Worker is not able to do his part, this program is hampered. DO IT WELL—IT IS FOR THE LORD.

Zone Program

The zone program has proved very effective in many localities adapted to this arrangement. The city is divided according to natural geographical lines and depending upon the number contained in a certain area. Sometimes different colored pins are attached to the zone map, designating addresses, prospects in that area, delinquent members, etc. The pins also help to determine at a glance the number in that zone. This program, as the alphabetical program, not only includes the young members of the church but the older ones also. It knits them closer together and keeps closer tabulation of their needs. This program could be emphasized to check on illnesses, deaths, for study periods, and spiritual problems. The elders should tell the zone leaders what they desire of these leaders. They should tell them to whom to report all illnesses, deaths and any spiritual problems. Zone leaders could be assigned virtually all those items listed in the alphabetical program —study it. Periodic meetings of these leaders will keep them posted on what is expected of them and they can work out some of their problems through such meetings. In large cities the zone program definitely has advantages over the alphabetical program. Following is printed a typical zoning of a town—this one deals with Shawnee, Oklahoma, my home town.

Zone Program

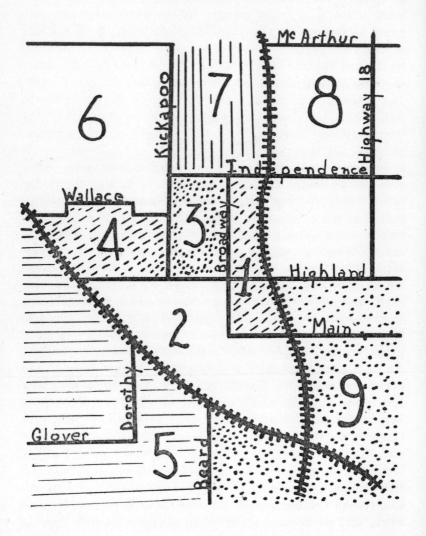

Office Procedure

The office procedure needs to be considered by all con-gregations for a number of reasons. An efficient well-kept office will assist greatly in the personal work program as well as all activities of a congregation. A nucleus of every congregation should be taught how to do personal work, and records in the office should provide the names of those that are adapted for training in this great work. The office procedure will give the names of the prospects with whom a follow-up program should be made and with whom appointments can be made. Too many congregations do not have any office procedure at all. Some do not even have a fellowship list (or membership list); some just do not realize its value, some think it might cost too much. The cost isn't high compared to the value. Office help may be acquired on a part-time or full time basis and either voluntary or paid—one or the other should be a must. When a congregation receives a letter, it is certainly good to have someone ready and able to answer that letter. Exchanging letters and ideas with other congregations, and answering letters promptly and efficiently helps to save more souls. If a prospect has been attending services and moves to another area, contact the closest congregation and suggest that someone visit that individual. An office should have a typewriter, filing cabinet and necessary machines and supplies. Some of the following forms are suggestive. Variations of these may be more helpful in some cases, while these forms may just give thought to other forms that might help in a particular situation. Now, just a further word about the office procedure. A horse that is not harnessed will not work, yet one that has on four sets of harness will not work well either— so do adopt the methods and forms suitable to your area of work, and do become efficient in keeping records, but do not become so encumbered and try to keep so many records that you lose sight of our goal: converting men and women to Christ. The tabs pictured at the top of the Office Personal Work Card are called Graffco Nu-Vise Signals and are available in twelve colors.

The procedure can be improved greatly with a few small helps. The forms help first, then the simple alphabetical filing, then tabbing some cards with numbers for quick key references, and different colors of cards. The message will easily distinguish the cards from each other, but the different colors cause them to be more easily recognized wherever they are. Any cards that have numbers at the top or letters at the bottom should have a master card at the front of the file, denoting what those letters or numbers are to designate—do not depend on your memory for this.

Visitor's Card

CHURCH OF CHRIST

Netherwood Park   Albuquerque, N. M.

Name: _____ Date: _____

Address: _____

Phone: _____

Church Affiliation: _____

I was invited by: Name: _____

Or by means of: Street Sign: _____ Other: _____

DEAR VISITOR: A cordial welcome is extended to you.- We desire to keep a record of all who visit with us. Please help us—
complete this card and drop it in the collection plate. Come and
study with us again.

(a)   (b)   c   d   e   f   g   (h)

Welcome   Office Personal   No further need because:
Card Sent   Work Card   1. Member of another congre-
                        Prepared ·   gation in the same area.
                                                 2. Do not live in area of the
                                                    congregation.

1. This card provides information from which to send a welcome card (next form) and to prepare an Office Personal Work Card (See later in this chapter).

2. Circle "a" when a welcome card is sent, circle "b" when an Office Personal Work Card is prepared, etc.

3. Procure visitor's cards from Bible School as well as worship Sunday morning and night.

4. Use the letters not circled for other designations as you desire.

Welcome Card

CHURCH OF CHRIST — NETHERWOOD PARK

5101 Indian School Road NE, Albuquerque, New Mexico

Phones: 5-8679 or 5-9967

We note that you were in our services recently, and this is to extend to you a hearty welcome to return and worship with us at any time you have the opportunity. If there is an aid or encouragement in the Christian life that any of us might extend on your behalf, please feel free to command us.

Sincerely,

Ivan R. Stewart, Evangelist.

---

1. The message on this card was taken from a card used at the Sixteenth and Decatur Streets Church, Washington, D. C.

2. Use the other side of this card for visitor's name and address, then stamp and mail.

Response Card

```
                         RESPONSE CARD
          Church of Christ—Netherwood Park, Albuquerque, New Mexico

          Name: _____
          Address: _____
          Date: _____ Phone: _____
          I desire to:
                        ☐  Be baptized.
                        ☐  Be restored by confessing my faults and asking
                           for the prayers of the church.
                        ☐  Be identified (If check here, —

          give last place of worship) _____
          Remarks: _____
                  (a)    (b)    c     d     e     f     g     h

     a  Letter of Encouragement sent                   b Office Personal Work Card
                                                          prepared
```

1. This card will provide the information for the church
   bulletin, welcome letter and preparation of the Office
   Personal Work Card, family record and follow up
   program.

OFFICE PERSONNEL WORK CARD

Members at local congregation
Delinquent Church Member
Prospect for Baptism
Needs Encouragement
Shut-In
Correspondence course sent
Placed membership with an- other congregation in the same area.
No further interest shown.
Moved out of town.
On Monthly (or current) vis- itation list.

| 1 | 2 | 3 | 4 | 5 | 6 | 7 | 8 | 9 | 10 |

OFFICE PERSONAL WORK CARD

Family
Name: _____ Tel: _____ Date: _____

Address: _____ Occ.: _____

| Given Name | Age | Church Affiliation |

H: _____

W: _____

1: _____

2: _____

3: _____

Where came from: _____

Invited by: Name: _____ Street Sign: _____ Other: _____

Members Volunteer to do: _____

Remarks: _____

This card should remain in the office files at all times.

1. This card (4 x 6) should be considered the master record.

2. If you use the zone system, zones can be noted by tabs on certain numbers.

3. The visitation list is made from this card from time to time.

4. Information obtained from the small personal work cards, after visits are completed, should be noted on the back of this card.

5. A guide card identifying tabs and numbers should be filed at the front of your cards for ready reference.

6. If 7-8-9 are circled, remove all other tabs and place in an alphabetical inactive card section.

7. This card prepared from one used by Brother Robert Hawkins.

Visitation List

A visitation list should be prepared at regular intervals, whether monthly, quarterly or semi-annually. The elders should determine the names to go on this list—the information can be obtained from the number 10 tab (if that one designated) on the Office Personal Work Card. Several sets of this list should be made, then the names can be cut and pasted on the card shown on the following page, yet keep at least one list not cut in the office. These cards can then be mailed to individuals at regular intervals who will visit the people indicated on the cards, or the cards could be passed out in classes, or handed out on the regular visitation night. At any rate, the person doing the visiting should certainly return the card with results of the visit noted—then this information will be posted on the back of the Office Personal Work Card which is kept in the office file at all times, and thus help in the follow up program. The following is a sample of a list prepared in Albuquerque—the names and addresses are fictitious, of course, but the information is real.

Visitation List

FEBRUARY 1955 VISITATION LIST

Name	Address	Telephone	Information
Mr. and Mrs. A	123 Robin Lane, NE	567	Visit [1] NP 11-21-54 Mr. [2] Bap. Mrs. Ch of Christ
Mrs. B	456 Wren Street NW	120	Visit NP off and on Ch of Christ
Mrs. C	789 Swallow Dr. SE	432	Del [3] Ch of Ch in Hospital — Farmington
Mr. D	012 Sparrow Lake Rd.	321	Mrs. Mem NP — Mr. Del Ch of Ch
Mr. E	123 Oriole Court	894	Mrs. Mem NP — Mr. ????
Mrs. F	434 Bluebird Way	543	Visit NP 8-54 & 2-55 Del Ch of Ch
Mr. & Mrs. G	730 Pigeon Drive	302	Mrs. Mem NP — Mr. ????
Mr. H	253 Thrush Lane	435	Mrs. Mem NP — Mr. Bap. — interested
Miss B	6789 Pelican Street	951	Del Ch Ch
Karen J (Child)	140 Finch Road	725	Att Bible School NP — Parents ????
Mr. & Mrs. K	235 Flamingo	174	Mrs. new convert — Mr. ????
Mr. & Mrs. L	490 Hawk Street	423	Mr. & Mrs. Christian Ch — visits off and on
Miss M (child)	753 Duck Lane	498	Child att Bible School — Parents No
Mr. N	321 Waxwing Drive	345	Visit NP 2-55
Mr. & Mrs. O	437 Hummingbird	203	Encourage Mrs. — Mr. Del Ch Ch
Mr. & Mrs. P	529 Blackbird Street	534	Mr.& Mrs. Att NP off & on — child Regular
Mr. & Mrs. Q	987 Woodthrush Court	765	Visit NP 12-19-54 — Mr. & Mrs. Bap.
Mr. R	506 Canary Lane	674	Enrolled [4] CC — Att off & on — Meth. Ch.

[1] Visited Local congregation November 21, 1954.

[2] Mr. is Baptist, Mrs. Church of Christ but not at local congregation.

[3] Delinquent Church of Christ Member.

[4] Enrolled in correspondence course.

Personal Work Card

```
    PERSONAL WORK CARD        Worker: _____

Name: _____

Address: _____ Tele: _____

Your remarks:




    Please write information concerning your personal visit or phone
    call or correspondence on front or back of this card and return to
    distributor or the church office.  Please return this card within one
    week from receipt.
```

1. Information from this card should be posted on the re-
   verse side of the Office Personal Work Card which is
   kept in the office files at all times.
2. These may be handed out in class or mailed. If mailed,
   the names of those who are willing to do this work can
   be secured from the Family Record card. If mailed, the
   following form should accompany this one.
3. This card can be destroyed after the information has
   been posted to the Office Personal Work Card or it
   may be filed.

Elder's Request For Visit

ELDER'S REQUEST FOR VISIT

To: _____

Since you have indicated on the Family Record your desire to make personal visits, we are requesting that you visit the persons indicated by the Personal Work card attached. It is our desire to have a written report on this visit within one week from the time you receive this.

1. Make this visit personal and warm.
2. Speak good — do not criticize.
3. Make the visit short — usually 15 to 20 minutes.
4. Offer to help in any way that will be beneficial.

_____
Elder requesting visit.

1. This is the Elder's request card and is self explanatory.

2. It should accompany the Personal Work Cards which may be given personally or mailed to the individuals the elders desire to make such visits.

Family Record Card

```
        1     2     3     4     5     6     7     8     9    10

                              FAMILY RECORD
                    Netherwood Park Church of Christ
                        Albuquerque, New Mexico
    Family Name _____Tel. _____ Date _____
    Address _____
              Given Name              Age   Church Affiliation   Occupation    Bus.Tel.
    Mr.   _____   ____   _____   _____   _____
    Mrs.  _____   ____   _____   _____   _____
    1.    _____   ____   _____   _____   _____
    2.    _____   ____   _____   _____   _____
    3.    _____   ____   _____   _____   _____
    Please check in appropriate squares those things members of your family are willing
    to do.  Indicate "other" by number from above.
    Mr. Mrs. Other                                                        Mr. Mrs. Other
    □      □   Lead Public Singing      Usher                              □      □
    □   □  □   Lead Class Singing       Assist at Lord's Supper            □      □
    □      □   Lead Public Prayer       Donate Blood. Type ____            □   □  □
    □      □   Make Announcements       Teach Bible Class                  □   □  □
    □      □   Preach                        What age? ____
    □      □   Read Scripture           Assist in Bible Class              □   □  □
    □   □  □   Visit sick in home            What age? ____
    □   □  □   Visit in hospital        Provide  Transportation            □   □  □
```

1. This is the front side of the Family Record Card. (4 x 6).

2. If you desire to know at a ready glance all who are willing to do
    a certain task (as leading singing, etc.) you could tab all num-
    ber 1's or some other number.

Family Record Card

Mr. Mrs. Other   Mr. Mrs. Other

☐ ☐ ☐ Teach in VBS   Telephone   ☐ ☐ ☐
☐ ☐ ☐ Assist in VBS   Home ____ Office ____   ☐ ☐ ☐
☐ ☐ ☐ Prepare clothes for needy   Work on bulletin   ☐ ☐ ☐
☐ ☐ ☐ Provide food for needy   Work on mimeographing   ☐ ☐ ☐
☐   Attend Men's Training Cl. Artistic work   ☐ ☐ ☐
   ☐   Attend Ladies' Bible Cl.   Building repair & cleaning   ☐ ☐ ☐
☐ ☐ ☐ Attend Personal Work Cl.   Do you have a Bible?
☐ ☐ ☐ Attend Sunday am Cl.   Yes ____ No ____
☐ ☐ ☐ Attend Sunday pm Cl.   Other:
☐ ☐ ☐ Attend Mid-week services
☐ ☐ ☐ Attend Gospel meetings
☐ ☐ ☐ See that children attend
       all classes—
☐ ☐ ☐ Type-Home ___ Office ___
       (Only check this if you
       have a typewriter)
☐ ☐ ☐ Make personals visits
       Day & time _____
☐ ☐ ☐ Address letters by hand
☐ ☐ ☐ Assist other office work

1. This is the back side of the Family Record Card. (4 x 6).

3. This card will provide many prospects with whom you may study—husbands, wives, children and relatives.

4. This card provides names of Christians willing to do visiting, etc.

5. This card provides information of prospective personal workers and many other services that can be rendered.

Enrollment Card — Correspondence Course

This is an actual reproduction of an enrollment card in the Correspondence Course entitled "Foundation Facts For Salvation" by Ivan R. Stewart—you may print or mimeograph cards similar to this.

CORRESPONDENCE COURSE

Name _____Mrs JKL_____ Age __40__

Street Address _____222 Hanford SE_____

City _____Albuquerque, New Mexico_____

Phone _____2-6540_____ Church Affiliation _____none_____

We are happy to have you study with us. The procedure is simple. Study each question and take your answer from the Bible references. Ask any questions you may have. If others in your family desire to study this course, request a separate series for each person. Encourage others to enroll in this study. Please fill out this card and return it with the first lesson. You will receive the second lesson with the graded lesson. The section below is for the teacher's purpose.

	Date Mailed	Date Received	Right	Wrong
Lesson 1	____Apr 22 1955____	____May 9 1955____	72	7
Lesson 2	____May 9 1955____	____Jun 7 1955____	62	8
Lesson 3	____Jun 7 1955____	____Jul 7 1955____	75	14
Lesson 4	____Jul 7 1955____	____Aug 8 1955____	70	4
Lesson 5	____Aug 8 1955____	____Sep 21 1955____	95	9
Lesson 6	——Sep 21 1955____	____Oct 4 1955____	68	0

Remarks: Last question "no"   Baptized 10-9-55
enrolled by:

This card (4 x 6) will provide names of interested parties with whom you may study. Such names should appear on the visitation list.

Enrollment Card

January				February				March				April			
1	2	3	4	1	2	3	4	1	2	3	4	1	2	3	4

ATTENDANCE RECORD

of

Name _____

Address _____

Telephone _____

_____ Teacher

_____ Class

CHURCH OF CHRIST — NETHERWOOD PARK
5101 Indian School Road N.E.
Albuquerque, New Mexico

(left margin: July 4 3 2 1 — August 4 3 2 1)
(right margin: May 1 2 3 4 — June 1 2 3 4)

September				October				November				December			
1	2	3	4	1	2	3	4	1	2	3	4	1	2	3	4

1. Prepare Office Personal Work Card from all enrollments in the Bible School.

2. Appointments with prospects can be made from these cards, (4 x 6), that is those who are enrolled but have not as yet obeyed the gospel.

Those

THOSE WHO SERVE

ON THE LORD'S DAY MORNING	FOR THE MONTH OF				
	FIRST	SECOND	THIRD	FOURTH	FIFTH
LORD'S SUPPER					
Announcer *					
Song Leader *					
Prayer Leader *					
Pray-Bread **					
Pray-Fruit Vine **					
Leader-Attendant					
Attendant					
Attendant					
Attendant					
Alerted					
Alerted					
USHERS					
Greet in Vestibule					
Door Man					
Center Aisle Man					
West Aisle Man					
East Aisle Man					
Alerted					
Benediction					

1. This list is prepared monthly.
2. New converts should be worked into the public service gradually.

e List

Song Leader ***

Prayer Leader ***

Lord's Table Leader

Lord's Table Attendant

Ushers — See Assignment made above — same in the evening services.

Benediction

* On the Rostrum at 10:45 a.m. ** On the Rostrum immediately after Sermon.

*** On the Rostrum at 5:00 p.m. or 7:00 p.m. whichever is appropriate.

ON WEDNESDAY EVENING

Song Leader

Prayer Leader

Benediction

Ushering

REMARKS:

1. Brother _____ will check the above list prior to each service. Please notify him at telephone _____ if it is known before hand that for some reason you will not be present.

2. Be sure, brethren, that you check carefully this list before each service, and thus be prepared to render the part assigned you for the following services, for the success of this program depends upon how faithfully each person keeps up with his assignment, and that without having to be reminded from time to time.

NOTE: Duplicate of this should be under the front bench at all times. This duplicate does not have to show all appointments (Mainly those to appear on the rostrum).

APPROVED:

_____ Virgil Cox, Elder _____ Erroll T. Gay, Elder _____ Wayne Stell, Elder

3. The desire to serve may be procured from the Family Record.
4. This form is adapted from one prepared by Robert Hawkins.

Bibliography

This bibliography is not presented because these are the books which were consulted in the preparation of this work, although it does include most of them. It is a bibliography given with the idea of helping the Personal Worker with his work, the doctrines of others and also books relative to the new convert. The list of books for the new convert is given in a suggested order of procurement.

BIBLIOGRAPHY FOR THE PERSONAL WORKER

Bible

You Can Do Personal Work, Otis Gatewood, published by Otis Gatewood, Los Angeles, California, 1945.

Let's Go Fishing for Men, Homer Hailey, published by Chronicle Publishing Company, Inc., Abilene, Texas, 1951.

Alleged Bible Contradictions, George DeHoff, published by DeHoff Publications, Murfreesboro, Tennessee, 1948.

Christian Evidences, J. W. McGarvey, published by The Christian Standard Publication Company, Cincinnati, Ohio.

Why We Believe the Bible, George DeHoff, published by DeHoff Publications, Murfreesboro, Tennessee, 1948.

Is the Bible The Word of God? W. Graham Scroggie, Moody Press, Chicago, Illinois, 1922.

He Took it upon Himself, Margaret Slattery, Pilgrim Press, Boston, Massachusetts, 1930.

Jesus The Master Teacher, Herman H. Horne, Associated Press, 1907.

A Fortune to Share, Vashni Young, Bobbs-Merrill Company, Indianapolis, Indiana, 1931.

How to Win Friends and Influence People, Dale Carnegie, Simon and Schuster, New York, New York, 1937.

Every Member Evangelism, J. E. Conant, Sunday School Times Company. Philadelphia, Pennsylvania, 1922.

Mere Christianity, Clive S. Lewis, MacMillan Company, New York, New York, 1952.

BIBLIOGRAPHY FOR LEARNING OF OTHERS DOCTRINES

His Many Mansions, Rulon S. Howells, Murray and Gee, Inc., Hollywood, California, 1944.

Churches of Today, L. G. Tomlinson, Gospel Advocate Company, Nashville, Tennessee, 1927.

Chaos of the Cults, Karl Van Baalens, Published by William B. Eerdmans, Grand Rapids, Michigan.

Ready Answers to Religious Errors, A. C. Williams and J. H. Dykes, Gospel Advocate Company, Nashville, Tennessee, 1946.

Manuals, Creeds, Disciplines and Catechisms containing practices and beliefs of the various religious groups.

BIBLIOGRAPHY FOR THE NEW CONVERT

Bible

Tract: Now that I am a Christian, R. B. Sweet.

Tract: Is Church Attendance Essential? A. G. Hobbs.

Some of the Gospel papers.

20th Century Christian, 3909 Granny White Pike, Nashville, Tenn.

Power For Today—for Daily Devotionals, published by the 20th Century Christian, 3909 Granny White Pike, Nashville, Tenn.

Why I am a Member of the Church of Christ, published by author, LeRoy Brownlow, Ft. Worth, Texas, 1945.

Why We Believe the Bible, George DeHoff, George DeHoff Publications, Murfreesboro, Tennessee, 1948.

Any good Bible Correspondence Course, One suggestion: Foundation Facts For Salvation, 6 lessons, Ivan R. Stewart.

Nichol's Pocket Encyclopedia, C. R. Nichol, published by C. R. Nichol, Clifton, Texas, 1949.

People's New Testament with Notes, B. W. Johnson, 2 Volumes, Christian Publishing Company, St. Louis, Missouri, 1889.

Cruden's Concordance, Alexander Cruden, The John C. Winston Company, Philadelphia, Pennsylvania, 1930.

Hurlbut's Storybook of the Bible, Jesse L. Hurlbut, The John C. Winston Company, Philadelphia, Pennsylvania, 1932.

Smith's Bible Dictionary, William Smith, Fleming H. Revell Company, New York, New York.

Clarke's Commentaries, Adam Clarke, Available any religious book store.

Most of these books suggested can be procured through book stores operated by members of the church of Christ. All that is written is not endorsed but will be most helpful in a study of the Bible. This last statement has to do especially with the last three books suggested.